Energizing Your Organization

OTHER BOOKS BY THE AUTHOR

Knowing the Truth about Education (2015)
Reality and Education: A New Direction for Educational Policy (2013)

Energizing Your Organization

The Ultimate School Work Environment

Daniel Wentland

ROWMAN & LITTLEFIELD
Lanham • Boulder • New York • London

Published by Rowman & Littlefield

A wholly owned subsidiary of The Rowman & Littlefield Publishing Group, Inc.
4501 Forbes Boulevard, Suite 200, Lanham, Maryland 20706
www.rowman.com

Unit A, Whitacre Mews, 26-34 Stannary Street, London SE11 4AB

Copyright © 2017 by Daniel Wentland

All rights reserved. No part of this book may be reproduced in any form or by any electronic or mechanical means, including information storage and retrieval systems, without written permission from the publisher, except by a reviewer who may quote passages in a review.

British Library Cataloguing in Publication Information Available

Library of Congress Cataloging-in-Publication Data is Available

ISBN: 978-1-4758-3149-8 (cloth: alk. paper)
ISBN: 978-1-4758-3150-4 (pbk: alk. paper)
ISBN: 978-1-4758-3151-1 (electronic)

Printed in the United States of America

Contents

Acknowledgments vii

Preface ix

Introduction xiii

PART I: THE ELEMENTS OF AN ULTIMATE SCHOOL WORK ENVIRONMENT 1

1 Fundamental Concepts 3

2 The Culture 9

3 Leadership 21

4 Effective Management 29

5 Completing the Leadership and Management Picture 35

PART II: MEASURING AN ULTIMATE SCHOOL WORK ENVIRONMENT 41

6 What Does an Ultimate School Work Environment Look Like? 43

7 Does Your School Measure Up? 57

8 Decision Time 63

Conclusion: Final Comment 71

Acknowledgments

First, I want to express my appreciation to the readers, I look forward to reading your comments on Amazon.com and other book review websites.

Next, a big thanks to Tom and his crew at Rowman & Littlefield for taking another chance with me.

Thanks to my editor Dr. Andrew Kelly.

On a personal note, I appreciate everything my dad did for me while he was on this planet.

Finally, my days are always brighter with Kathy, Dakota, Scarlett, and Hailey.

Preface

The following tale is from *Zapp! The Lightening of Empowerment* by William Byham and Jeff Cox (1988):

> Ralph worked in Department N of the Normal Company in Normalburg, USA.
> As you might expect, just about everything was normal at Normal, including the understanding of who was normally supposed to do what:
> Managers did the thinking
> Supervisors did the talking
> And employees did the doing
> Ralph was your normal type of employee. He came to work. He did the job his supervisor told him to do. And at the end of the day he dragged himself home to get ready to do it all again.
> When friends or family asked him how he liked his work, Ralph would say, "Oh, it's all right, I guess. Not very exciting, but I guess that's normal. Anyway, it's a job and the pay is OK."
> In truth, working for the Normal Company was not very satisfying for Ralph, though he was not sure why. The pay was more than OK; it was good. The benefits were fine, the working conditions were safe. Yet something seemed to be missing.
> But Ralph figured there wasn't much he could do to change things at Normal. After all, he reasoned, who would even bother to listen? So at work he kept his thoughts to himself, and just did what he was told.

The Normal Company is typical of many organizations including schools, an okay place to work, but certainly not an ultimate workplace. In schools like the Normal Company, employees summarize their employment situation by stating, "There are worse places to work."

As a researcher, I spend my time formulating principles designed to enhance the performance of organizations by establishing an effective and efficient workplace.

On the other hand, practitioners have the ability to implement policies, practices, theories, and so forth. A critical question for practitioners is what workflow processes and policies have been implemented in the workplace and would the stakeholders associated with your organization describe your institution as an ultimate work environment as well as an effective and efficient organization?

In the K-12 environment, the primary form of an organization is a school or school district. And unfortunately the vast majority of schools or school districts operate like the Normal Company.

To move away from a Normal Company workplace requires a school or school district to adopt the elements of the ultimate school work environment. These elements are the ingredients that will make your school or school district a more productive work environment; make no mistake about it, developing a more productive work environment and gaining a competitive advantage can be the difference between organizational sustainability and maximizing or minimizing the learning that occurs within your school or school district.

By the way, ultimate work environments are quite rare, and when you find one you know it, for it's like a beautiful sparkling diamond. All the employees shine with an enthusiasm that can't be contained for they understand the unique environment in which they work.

Never forget the truism that "people respond to what is around them" (Crosby, 1986, p. 179); the information in this book will help every reader understand what it truly means to develop an ultimate school work environment.

Achieving greatness requires great achievements and the issue becomes how greatness can be best achieved in the learning environment—the Normal Company approach[1] or the ultimate school workplace approach?

Another point of clarification, for the remainder of the book, only the term "school" will be referred to. The term "school district" will not be mentioned again; however all the concepts presented in the book can be utilized at the school district level.

By the way, school districts that create an ultimate school work environment in every school will obtain educational outcomes that far exceed other school districts; just like an extraordinary racehorse can leave the rest of the field in a cloud of dust as it gallops ahead of them to victory after victory.

NOTE

1. For the remainder of the book, the term "Normal School approach" will be substituted for the term "Normal Company approach." Both terms refer to the workplace described at the beginning of the preface. The term "Normal School approach" is more applicable to the educational arena.

REFERENCES

Byham, W. C. & J. Cox. (1988). *Zapp! The Lightening of Empowerment.* New York: Fawcett Columbine Book, pp. 3–4.

Crosby, P. B. (1986). *Running Things: The Art of Making Things Happen.* New York: Mentor, p. 179.

Introduction

Creating an ultimate school work environment is generally about crafting a workplace built upon striving for excellence, developing collaboration, fostering trust, respecting all, and rewarding merit at the individual, group,* and organizational level.**

However, underneath everything, we must never forget that an ultimate school work environment is first and foremost all about the people who work in the school. How the administrators and non-administrative employees relate to one another impacts the morale of the workforce and the effort that each employee is willing to exert.

Have you ever worked for a school where it felt like no one cared about you and that your contribution to the school was always minimized or worse, unappreciated? Unfortunately, I have worked for many institutions where senior officials thought they were the greatest things on earth and everyone else was there to do their bidding. Working for a school like that can be labeled dispiriting, to say the least.

In contrast, being employed in a school where each employee understands the important role that he or she plays is a powerful factor that separates effective schools from mediocre and plain bad places to work.

In this book, the chapters are designed to move us toward a complete understanding of what an ultimate school work environment is, how to develop such an environment, and how to measure whether your school is an ultimate school workplace.

The writing is concise and straightforward and leads us on a journey of how to increase the probability of organizational effectiveness and develop a better awareness of who we are, for not every person wants to create an ultimate school work environment.

Many school decision-makers and educational practitioners talk about developing an ultimate school work environment, but few actually move beyond the talk. It is very common for individuals in positions of power to make statements about how great it is to work in the school while the rest of the employees know the "real" work situation.

So let's start our journey of moving beyond words and discover what it takes to turn words into reality and actually transform your school into an ultimate school work environment.

A REMINDER

* For our purposes, a group refers to academic departments such as the math department or English department and so forth.

** The organizational level refers to the entire school.

Part I

THE ELEMENTS OF AN ULTIMATE SCHOOL WORK ENVIRONMENT

Do no harm

—Peter Drucker's advice cited by Twomey, Jennings, & Fox (2005, p. 49)

Chapter One

Fundamental Concepts

Broadly, the term *organization* refers to a group of people working together to attain common goals. Researchers have tried to understand the nature of an organization by utilizing a variety of descriptions and analytical approaches, a summary of which is contained in my previous books, *Strategic Training: Putting Employees First* and *Organizational Performance in a Nutshell*.

For this book, we can simply state that from the body of research devoted to studying organizational development, three common elements have been cited to describe an organization: (1) people, (2) a goal or purpose, and (3) a structure (meaning any phenomena created by the members of an organization) that defines roles and positions, processes and limits the behavior of members of an organization.

Put simply, without people, a goal or purpose, and some form of structure, there is no organization! Of the three elements of an organization, *people* constitute the most important factor, because without human beings, the other two elements cease to exist.

People are the most important element of an organization.

Once the three elements of an organization are brought together and an organization is formed, a culture develops. Two of the most comprehensive definitions of organizational culture are listed below:

> The pattern of basic assumptions that a given group has invented, discovered, or developed in learning to cope with its problems of external adaptation and internal integration. (Schein, 1983, p. 14)

A set of symbols, ceremonies, and myths that communicate the underlying values and beliefs of that organization to its employees. (Ouchi, 1981, p. 41)

Organizational culture is important because numerous books and studies have demonstrated that the culture of an organization impacts organizational success or failure; therefore, the critical question is what type of organizational culture or work environment will best support organizational sustainability?

If we define sustainability as the "capacity of a system to engage in the complexities of continuous improvement consistent with deep values of human purpose" (Fullan, 2005, p. IX) and consider a Normal School approach as described in the preface or developing an ultimate school work environment, it becomes obvious which approach can better achieve organizational sustainability as well as organizational greatness.

Creating an ultimate school work environment can elevate a school above the competition by creating a more productive workforce and reaping all the organizational advantages and benefits that flow from a knowledgeable, highly skilled, and motivated workforce. The issue now becomes how to craft an ultimate school work environment.

The issue is how to develop an ultimate school work environment.

THE BUILDING BLOCKS OF AN ULTIMATE SCHOOL WORK ENVIRONMENT

Developing an ultimate school work environment begins with the notion of a norm of reciprocity. Gouldner (1960) suggested that a norm of reciprocity imposes two interrelated demands. The first is that people should help those individuals who helped them and secondly, people should not injure individuals who have helped them.

Similarly social exchange theory posits that individuals will demonstrate greater commitment to an organization when they feel supported and fairly rewarded. In other words, individuals will form relationships with those who can provide valued resources and in exchange those individuals will reciprocate by providing their resources and support (Umback, 2007).

Norm of Reciprocity

Social Exchange Theory

Another concept at the heart of an ultimate school work environment is the economic idea of an efficiency wage. An efficiency wage is a wage higher than the wage which equates quantity supplied and quantity demanded or it is a wage higher than the market clearing wage, or as economists would state, an efficiency wage is a wage higher than the equilibrium wage.

An Efficiency Wage

Generally, an organization would decide to pay an efficiency wage to lower overall labor costs. How can an organization reduce overall labor costs by paying a higher wage?

- First, fewer workers will be required to produce output.
- Second, workers increase their work effort because they do not want to lose their job because similar alternative employment positions will pay less.
- Third, an organization will experience a lower employee turnover rate and therefore reduce the costs associated with hiring and training employees.
- Finally, an organization can be more selective in terms of a worker's knowledge, skills, and abilities. An organization that pays an efficiency wage can hire better qualified workers, meaning the employees are more knowledgeable, highly skilled, and more capable of performing the job.

The bottom line is the more productive an employee is, the less inefficient the worker is.

The final result is higher output at lower overall costs.

As stated by Ari Haseotes, the president and chief operating officer of Cumberland Farms, when turnover is high, customer satisfaction suffers (Weber, 2013). When turnover is high, employee costs increase, employee performance is diminished, customer service is provided at a minimum level at best, and organizational sustainability and greatness is in serious jeopardy.

A Clarification Regarding an Efficiency Wage

For clarification purposes, if all organizations offered an efficiency wage, the positive effects of providing an efficiency wage would be negated with the end result being higher unemployment because wages above the equilibrium or market clearing wage always creates unemployment. However, for strategic, economic, and other managerial reasons, not all organizations will pay an efficiency wage; thus the organizations that do can reap all the economic and organizational benefits associated with paying an efficiency wage.

Besides an efficiency wage, merit pay at the individual, group,* and organizational level** is a critical component of an ultimate school work environment. How many of us have worked at an institution where employee performance really did not matter? Whether your work was outstanding and far superior to that of others or whether you did the minimum that was required, or something less than the minimum, all employees basically received the same pay increase.

John Kenneth Galbraith once said, "I am puzzled as to why a merit system is important in the absence of merit," (Galbraith & Goodman 1998, p. 72). Employee performance is a critical element impacting organizational success and employee performance at the individual, group,* and organizational level** must be rewarded according to effort exerted. Keep in mind that merit pay by itself does not reflect an ultimate school work environment; however, it is a necessary ingredient of an ultimate school workplace.

Merit Pay

THE RIGHT ACTION PRINCIPLE

Norm of reciprocity, social exchange theory, efficiency wage, and merit pay at the individual, group,* and organizational level** are encapsulated within the right action principle. An ultimate school work environment is built upon the right action principle meaning that pursuing organizational goals and objectives should be conducted in such a manner that growth and the integrity of people are respected (Johnston, 1994 cited by Seyfarth, 2005).

The Right Action Principle

I will modify the right action principle and state that the concept means never attempting to achieve organizational goals at the expense of the employees. Put simply, organizations that plan every action around their employees increase the probability of thriving as opposed to organizations that view employees as mere costs to be reduced in times of trouble.

Making the right action principle the cornerstone of your school culture, strategy, structure, processes, and policies is a key test of whether your school can ever be an ultimate school work environment. Unfortunately most schools fail the test.

The Right Action Principle Should Be the Fundamental Principle of a School's Culture.

Unfortunately, Most Schools Don't Measure Up.

SUMMING IT UP

A number of persons or groups united for some purpose of work expresses the essential character of an organization. "The participants, to one degree or another, have submitted to the purposes of organization in pursuit of some common purpose, which then normally involves the winning of the submission of people or groups external to the organization" (Galbraith, 1983, p. 55).

An ultimate school work environment increases the probability of winning the submission of people or groups internal and external to the school. In other words, ultimate school work environments are better able to attract and retain loyal internal and external stakeholders and as a result are in a more competitive position to increase the probability of achieving positive educational outcomes.

An Ultimate School Work Environment

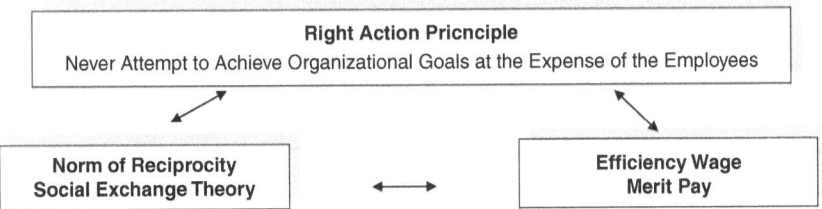

A REMINDER

* For our purposes, a group refers to academic departments such as the math department or English department and so forth.

** The organizational level refers to the entire school.

REFERENCES

Fullan, M. (2005). *Leadership & Sustainability: System Thinkers in Action.* Thousand Oaks, CA: Corwin Press/Sage Publications Company.

Galbraith, J. K. (1983). *The Anatomy of Power.* Boston, MA: Houghton Mifflin Company, p. 55.

Galbraith, J. K. & J. Goodman (eds.). (1998). Letters *to Kennedy.* Cambridge, MA: Harvard University Press, p. 72.

Gouldner, A. W. (1960). The Norm of Reciprocity: A Preliminary Statement. *American Sociological Review*, 25, pp. 161–177.

Johnston, B. (1994). Educational administration in the postmodern age. In S. Maxcy, (Ed.) Postmodern school leadership: Meeting the crisis in educational administration (pp. 115–131). Westport, CT: Praeger

Ouchi, W. G. (1981). *Theory Z: How American Business Can Meet the Japanese Challenge.* Reading, MA: Addison-Wesley, p. 41.

Schein, E. (Summer 1983). The Role of the Founder in Creating Organizational Culture. *Organizational Dynamics,* p. 14.

Seyfarth, J. T. (2005). *Human Resources Management for Effective Schools* (4th Ed.). Boston, MA: Pearson/Allyn and Bacon, p. 109.

Twomey, D., M. Jennings, & I. Fox. (2005). Anderson's *Business Law and the Legal Environment* (Standard Volume, 19th Ed.). Mason, OH: Thompson-South-Western, p. 49.

Umback, P. D. (Winter 2007). How Effective are they? Exploring the Impact of Contingent Faculty on Undergraduate Education. *The Review of Higher Education*, 30(2), pp. 91–123.

Weber, L. (June 11, 2013). What Makes Staff Stay Longer? Here's One Company's Answer. *Wall Street Journal,* p. B3.

Chapter Two

The Culture

In the first chapter we examined the fundamental concepts of an ultimate school work environment. However, to fully comprehend what constitutes an ultimate school work environment we must venture forward by introducing the additional elements of such a unique workplace. Our first step in that direction begins with an analysis of a school organizational culture "A" work environment.

A school organizational culture "A" workplace is part of an ultimate school work environment.

To gain an insight into the dynamics of a school organizational culture "A" workplace we must think of an organization as a system consisting of a group of interrelated or interacting elements forming a unified whole that works toward a common goal by accepting inputs and producing outputs in an organized transformation process.

A dynamic system essentially has three basic interacting components or functions: an input function that involves capturing and assembling elements that enter the system to be processed; a processing element or transformation process that converts an input into an output; and the output that has been produced.

A Dynamic System

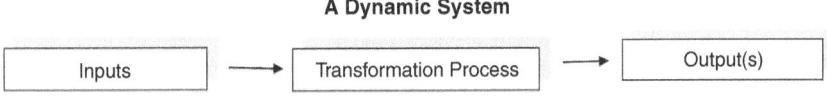

A cybernetic system includes two additional components: feedback and control. Feedback is the data about the performance of a system. Control involves monitoring and evaluating feedback to determine whether or not a system is moving toward the achievement of its goal(s).

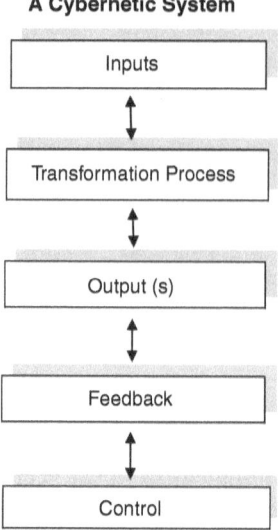

A Cybernetic System

In addition, a system can either be classified as an open system or an adaptive system.

An open system is a system that interacts with other systems in its environment. An adaptive system has the ability to change itself or its environment in order to survive.

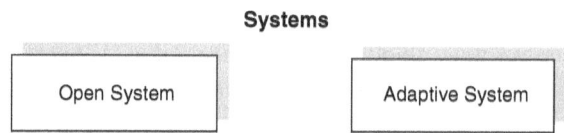

Systems

Every organization has all three components: input, processing, and output. An effective and efficient organization has all five system components working together as a harmonious whole while having the capacity to interact with other systems and successfully adapt to any environmental change. If your school is underperforming, it is the systems that have been established within the school that are producing those poor results.

Unsuccessful schools are dysfunctional systems. To correct the situation, those systems must be either modified or abandoned, in which case new systems will need to be developed.

SYSTEMS AND ORGANIZATIONAL CULTURE

Impacting the systems within an organization is the culture of the institution. Organizational culture is a primary factor that explains why one organization succeeds while another entity fails, even though both organizations are producing similar outputs.

To delve deeper into a school culture, we can use three workplace parameters to help us create a framework for measuring four distinct school organizational cultures. These four school organizational cultures, in turn, set the stage for the development of the Organizational Culture Educational Status Model (OCESM).

This model can be used to classify and, more importantly, predict the quality of the learning environment of a school based on its culture, with the ultimate objective of developing a course of action that will improve the culture of a school and thus its learning environment.

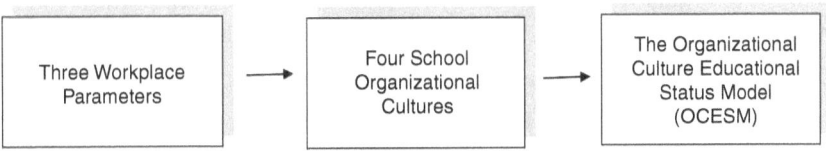

The OCESM is a flexible analytical tool that opens the door to a new perspective of research regarding the quantification of organizational culture by offering a framework for predicting the quality of the learning environment of a school based on the culture of the school, ceteris paribus.

Once we explain the model, we will highlight the connection between organizational culture and the "people factor" within a school. Ultimately, it's the quality of the people within a school that will determine the effectiveness of the learning environment.

SETTING THE STAGE FOR THE OCESM: WORKPLACE PARAMETERS

The first workplace parameter is administrative attitudes and practices in the workplace. Those attitudes can be assessed by the overall degree of trust or lack of trust between administrative and nonadministrative personnel. An adversarial relationship between administrative and nonadministrative personnel tends to develop when management focuses too much on operational and noneducational issues while ignoring or paying limited attention to the well-being of employees.

Dissatisfied employees purposely engage in many behaviors that limit productivity and compromise school success. A fertile breeding ground for advancing productivity and promoting organizational success can only be laid when individuals are respected for who they are and placed in positions that complement their strengths. And make no mistake about it: Increasing productivity is the driving force behind an effective school and establishing a positive learning environment.

William J. Baumol and Alan S. Blinder in their 2000 book *Economics: Principles and Policies* put it this way:

> Only rising productivity can raise standards of living in the long run. Over long periods of time, small differences in rates of productivity growth compound like interest in a bank account and can make an enormous difference to a society's prosperity.

From a strict organizational perspective, the right administrative attitude can breathe life into a management philosophy or culture that will boost the chances of organizational success by establishing a workplace environment in which individuals will want to consistently perform at their best.

The First Workplace Parameter

Trust Between Administrators and Nonadministrative Employees

The second workplace parameter is the organizational environment among the employees. This environment can be assessed by examining the extent of cooperation and internal politics and favoritism within the school. A highly politicized work environment will eat away at collegiality and undermine productivity. If left unchecked, it will eventually squelch innovation, cripple productivity, and minimize educational outcomes.

The long-term effectiveness of a school and the quality of the learning environment will depend on whether or not it controls internal politics and favoritism. Any school that fails to base performance and compensation on merit will drift into mediocrity. Merit must be rewarded; favoritism must be discouraged.

The Second Workplace Parameter

A Non-politicized Work Environment

The third workplace parameter is the tasks being performed within a school. These tasks can be assessed by asking whether or not they have meaning for the individuals performing them. Individuals tend to be more productive when they sense that their work means something and that they "mean something," and when they feel that their school is making a positive impact on society.

The recent Atlanta School District cheating episode and seemingly endless string of company and government agency scandals illustrate the negative impact of organizational cultures that foster unethical behavior. Organizations involved in unethical behavior tend to experience short-term, and in many situations, long-term deterioration in employee performance.

On the other hand, organizations that create an environment where individuals feel that their work is important and that their organization is providing a positive benefit to the community set the stage for innovation and creativity. When innovation and creativity flourish, so will productivity—the driving force behind effective schools and positive educational outcomes.

The Third Workplace Parameter

Work Tasks and Ethical Behavior

How Do We Measure a School Organizational Culture?

Using the three critical workplace parameters of attitude, environment, and tasks, we can establish criteria for measuring four distinct school organizational cultures. Then we can assess the learning environment associated with the four distinct school organizational cultures.

Administrative Attitudes and Practices

Individuals tend to trust the administration when operational and non-educational topics and employee satisfaction issues are given equal attention by administrators.

Individuals tend to distrust the administration when administrators focus on operational and non-educational topics yet ignore employee satisfaction issues or give them only limited attention.

The Organizational Environment

The ideal environment is one in which cooperation among individuals and groups* is encouraged, politicking and favoritism are discouraged, and performance and compensation issues are based on merit.

An atmosphere of non-cooperation exists when cooperation among individuals and groups* is discouraged, politicking and favoritism are encouraged, and performance and compensation issues are not based on merit.

The Tasks Being Performed

The task has meaning to the individual when he or she feels that his or her actions have a meaningful impact on the school. The individual should feel that the school stands for something more than cost minimization—that it also contributes to the welfare of the community. In addition, the school must pursue ethical behavior in accomplishing its educational goals and strategic objectives.

Tasks do not have meaning if individuals feel that their actions have no meaningful impact on the school, the school is primarily focused on minimizing costs, and the school allows unethical actions to occur.

With our measurement criteria established, we can now see four distinct school organizational cultures:

```
Four School Organizational Cultures

            Culture A

            Culture C

            Culture D

            Culture F
```

School Organizational Culture "A"
- There is a relationship of trust between administrative and non-administrative personnel.
- Cooperation between individuals and groups* is encouraged, and politicking and favoritism are discouraged. Performance and compensation issues are based on merit.
- Individuals feel that their actions have a meaningful impact on the school. And that their school stands for more than cost minimization, has a positive impact upon the community and operates in an ethical manner.

School Organizational Culture "C"
- Two of the three elements of school organizational culture "A" are present (e.g., trust and cooperation). However, the tasks might not have meaning for the individual.

School Organizational Culture "D"
- One of the three elements of school organizational culture "A" is present (e.g., the tasks might have meaning for the individual, but there is no trust or cooperation present within the culture of the school).

School Organizational Culture "F"
- None of the three elements of school organizational culture "A" are present

Now that we have identified four measurable and distinct school organizational cultures, we can present the OCESM.

According to the OCESM:

- Schools that have a type "A" culture are predicted to outperform other schools using standard educational measurements of organizational and student performance. As for policy recommendations, the OCESM suggests that administrative personnel should continue with their current practices.

Schools that have a type "A" organizational culture will outperform other schools, ceteris paribus

---

- Schools that have a type "C" culture are predicted to have higher educational outcomes as compared to type "D" or "F" schools. The policy recommendation for these schools is to incorporate within their school culture the missing school organizational culture "A" element, and thus form a type "A" culture.

Schools that have a type "C" organizational culture need to become a type "A" school

---

- Schools that have a type "D" culture are predicted to perform significantly below type "A" or "C" schools. The policy recommendation for these schools is to develop a type "C" school organizational culture in the short-run then a type "A" school organizational culture in the long-run.

> **Schools with a type "D" organizational culture are unacceptable**

- Schools that have a type "F" culture are predicted to perform significantly below type "A," "C," or "D" schools. The policy recommendation for these schools is to develop a type "D" school organizational culture in the short-run, then a "C" school organizational culture and finally an "A" school organizational culture in the long-run.

> **Schools with a type "F" organizational culture need a new administrative team to significantly improve the organizational culture and the learning environment**

THE OCESM AND THE BOTTOM LINE

The Organizational Cultural Educational Status Model, OCESM, links the culture of a school and the quality of the learning environment provided by a school. In addition, the model provides decision makers with a methodology to improve educational outcomes by adopting an administrative philosophy that fosters a type "A" school organizational culture.

The OCESM elevates the analysis regarding organizational culture by quantifying the culture of a school in order to predict the quality of the learning environment, while also providing a course of action to improve the organizational culture of a school. In the final analysis, providing a quality learning environment is what education should be all about!

> **Education should be about providing a quality learning environment**

THE OCESM AND THE "PEOPLE FACTOR"

School organizational cultures "A," "C," "D," and "F" provide a framework for understanding school performance—a framework built on three critical workplace parameters: administrative attitudes and practices in the workplace; the organizational environment among the employees; and the tasks being performed within an a school.

At the core of the OCESM lies a common thread that binds each of the three critical workplace parameters together. This common thread is the driving force that ultimately determines whether or not a school will possess an "A," "C," "D," or "F" school organizational culture. So what is this common thread? The "people" element is the most important factor in any organization.

In sum, the quality of an organization's people, at all levels, determines organizational success or failure because an organization is nothing more than the system(s) that the members of the organization created, and the superiority of any creation ultimately depends on the abilities of its creator(s). Thus, at the core of organizational performance is the quality of the members of an organization. Failing to recognize this truism leaves the organization in peril.

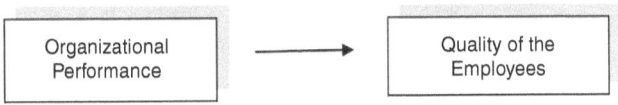

From an educational perspective, administrators that place themselves above the employees will never create an educational environment that maximizes learning.

Putting Employees First

In association with the OCESM and a school organizational culture "A" work environment is my employment principle of putting employees first.

In a *Wall Street Journal* article, it was reported that most organizations do not practice what they preach, despite the claims of a majority of executives that their organizations treat employees with respect and offer fair pay for the tasks performed (Kent, 2005).

The disconnection between what organizations say they believe and what they actually do is partly attributable to a marketing philosophy that began to dominate management theory after the production concept faded in popularity in the 1950s–1960s. At the center of this philosophy is the notion that the customer should be the focus of all organizational activities and planning.

Although the emphasis upon the customer appears to be a logical premise for building organizational success, it is actually quite misleading: Simply put, many organizations do not know who their customers are! For example, who is the customer at a college or university? High school graduates? Adults returning to college? Graduate students? Individuals from other countries attending classes? Or individuals seeking a vocational trade? And what is the socio-economic and demographic data associated with these classifications of students?

Who is the customer for a retailer like Wal-Mart? Is it the person who drives a Mercedes to Wal-Mart in order to purchase everyday items at lower prices? Or is it the individual who uses public transportation to arrive at the store? A customer who cannot be specifically identified in every detail is an illusion, and illusions serve as a poor basis for building successful strategy.

And once the "customer" has been identified, should he or she be placed at the center of every organizational activity? Doing so, I believe, pushes aside the true essence of the organization, minimizing its significance.

Should "the customer" be the focus of an organization?

No, the employees should be.

The heart of an organization is its employees (administrative and non-administrative). The abilities, decisions, plans, training, and actions of the employees of an organization are what draw individuals to a particular college or retailer or even to purchase a product or pay for a service. The primary driving force that brings people into a concert hall is to hear enchanting music performed by trained musicians whose skills and talents are on display. Highly qualified employees produce quality products and provide quality service that satisfies consumer needs.

An organization's employees have always made the difference between a truly successful organization and a mediocre entity, but it's amazing how often administrators overlook or discount this fundamental recipe for organizational effectiveness.

My premise here is that an organization that plans every action around its employees will thrive. The Wegman's chain of grocery stores headquartered in Rochester, New York, has repeatedly been cited as one of the best employers in the United States to work for. The company's focus on its employees has made Wegman's a shining example of a local, family-managed organization that effectively and efficiently competes against national and international grocery chains.

**The employees have always made the difference
in terms of organizational success**

THE ORGANIZATIONAL CULTURE EDUCATIONAL STATUS MODEL (OCESM)

The Organizational Culture Educational Status Model (OCESM)

School Organizational Culture "A"

Measurement Criteria: Trust exists, Cooperation is present, Task has meaning
Educational Learning Environment: Higher educational performance compared to other schools
Recommended Course of Action: Continue present policies and practices

---

School Organizational Culture "C"

Measurement Criteria: Two of the three elements of school organizational culture "A" are present
Educational Learning Environment: Better educational performance compared to Type "D" or Type "F" schools
Recommended Course of Action: Incorporate the missing element of school organizational culture "A" into the "C" culture

---

School Organizational Culture "D"

Measurement Criteria: one of the three elements of school organizational culture "A" is present
Educational Learning Environment: Educational performance significantly below Type "A" and "C" schools
Recommended Course of Action: Incorporate the two missing elements of school organizational culture "A" into the "D" culture

---

School Organizational Culture "F"

Measurement Criteria: Distrust, Non-cooperation, Task does not have meaning
Educational Learning Environment: The lowest educational performance compared to Type "A," "C," and "D" schools
Recommended Course of Action: Incorporate the three missing elements of school organizational culture "A" into the "F" culture

SUMMING IT UP

Developing a school organizational Culture "A" workplace and putting employees first are underlying foundations of an ultimate school work environment. As stated by Randy Best, "We believe that success in any venture, for profit or not profit, depends on the quality of people" (Manzo, 2006, p. 20).

A REMINDER

* For our purposes, a group refers to academic departments such as the math department or English department and so forth.
** The organizational level refers to the entire school.

REFERENCES

Baumol, W. J. & A. S. Blinder. (2000). *Economics: Principles and Policy*. Orlando, FL: Harcourt College Publishers.

Kent, S. (September 6, 2005). Happy Workers Are the Best Workers. *Wall Street Journal*, p. A20.

Manzo, K. (October 25, 2006). Voyager Sails into Market for Reading. *Education Week*, pp. 1 & 20.

Chapter Three

Leadership

Let's pause to recap before moving on. At this point in our journey, we have come to realize that an ultimate school work environment has its roots firmly embedded within the human relations notion of a norm of reciprocity, social exchange theory, and the economic principles of an efficiency wage and merit pay.

However, just as all the matter in the universe originated from the big bang, the primordial beginning of an ultimate school workplace is the right action principle. Additionally, an ultimate school work environment must foster a type "A" school organizational culture and embrace the managerial philosophy of putting employees first.

The bottom line from everything that has been exposed so far is that an ultimate school work environment requires a different perspective about what is important in order to achieve organizational greatness and sustain an effective learning environment.

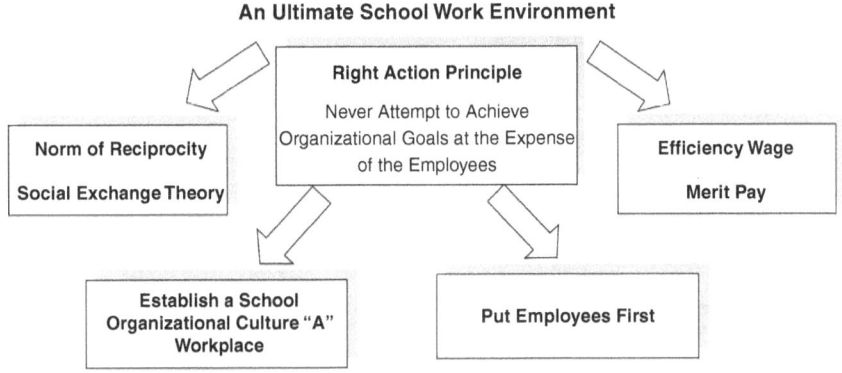

To be frank, talking about being an ultimate school workplace and really creating one are two very different circumstances; talk is cheap, actions are what count

In the management literature there is the notion of "X" and "Y" employees. Generally, X-type employees are viewed as lazy and management needs to constantly watch over the employees to make sure that something gets done while Y-type employees are eager to work and require minimum supervision.

Douglas McGregor's
Theory X and Theory Y

The same idea can be applied to management, there are "X" and "Y" leaders and administrators. X-type leaders and administrators are controlling and self-absorbed among other negative managerial tendencies while Y-type leaders and administrators are the opposite. As we will soon see, in a workplace supervised by X-type leaders and administrators the life blood of an ultimate school workplace is drained away, just like a vampire sucking the life out of a victim. An ultimate school work environment will never exist under the same roof where X-type leaders and administrators exist.

An Ultimate School Work Environment
Must Have Y-type Leaders and Administrators

Let's consider two individuals.

First Individual	Second Individual
• Highly materialistic • Always focused upon his needs • Not concerned about how goals are achieved as long as they are accomplished • Only concerned with the here and now • Insensitive toward the physical environment; meaning at the macro level, the Earth and at the micro level, the workplace • Not interested in anyone else's point of view • Power driven • Constantly favoring certain individuals	Has the opposite characteristics

Which individual would you prefer as a boss? I don't believe anyone of us would select the first individual and if you were unfortunate enough to have to work for a person like that how much effort do you put forth? The first individual has the characteristics associated with an egocentric view of life.

The second person has adopted an altruistic view of life. The right type of leader (Y-type leader or administrator) must possess an altruistic perspective of life for only that kind of person will have the characteristics that are necessary to inspire others to want to do their best.

An egocentric person is primarily consumed with satisfying his or her own needs. An altruistic person focuses upon the interests of others and as a result gains the trust and loyalty of those who work for him or her. It is that bond of trust and loyalty between the altruistic leader and the employees that sets the foundation for obtaining extraordinary organizational results.

Put simply, in terms of achieving organizational greatness and sustaining an effective learning environment an individual with an egocentric approach to life will in the long run never measure up to a person with an altruistic viewpoint.

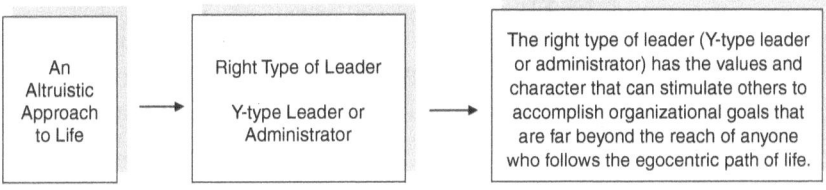

But what exactly is leadership? Unfortunately a straight forward description has proven elusive for leadership has been described in many ways by many individuals. Below are several generic descriptions of leadership:

- Leadership is the process whereby one person influences others to work toward a goal.
- Leadership is the process of guiding and motivating others toward the achievement of organizational goals.
- Strategic leadership refers to the ability to articulate a strategic vision and to motivate others to buy into that vision.
- Leadership is the ability to influence a group toward the achievement of goals.
- Leadership is the ability to get other people to get the very best out of themselves.
- Leadership is getting others to pursue a vision.
- Leadership is getting others to join you.

And the list can go on and on, but in the end, the description isn't important. What matters is that you are the right type of leader, a Y-type leader or administrator.

The Characteristics of the Right Type of Leader (Y-type Leader or Administrator)
Guided by the right action principle.
Has the right self-image and self-concept to want to create an ultimate school work environment in which the traditional management-employee relationship paradigm is cast aside in favor of a management-employee paradigm where employees are regarded as partners not subordinates; in other words the right type of leader (Y-type leader or administrator) puts employees first.
Administration retains the final decision-making authority but the focus should be upon how school decisions impact the employees, for that in turn will influence how the employees perform their jobs and ultimately impacts the effectiveness of the school in terms of achieving sustainable, positive educational outcomes.
Is sociable, conscientious, tactful, considerate, and open to various points of view.
Is not focused upon what he or she can gain but instead is concerned about the conditions of all those individuals who work for him or her. By truly caring about the employees, the right type of leader (Y-type leader or administrator) will achieve unparalleled organizational success.
In other words, the right type of leader (Y-type leader or administrator) makes a true commitment to the employees and it's that commitment that inspires the employees to want to accomplish organizational goals in the most effective and efficient manner (social exchange theory).
Embraces change, whether it is small or large, whenever it is necessary to do so. In fact the right type of leader (Y-type leader or administrator) actively promotes a school organizational culture that has an enhanced capacity to learn, adapt, and change.
The right type of leader (Y-type leader or administrator) must possess an altruistic perspective of life, for only that kind of person has the characteristics to inspire others to want to do their best.

Now let's compare the characteristics of the right type of leader (Y-type of leader or administrator) with a leadership style that flows from an egocentric perspective of life and can best be described as a CREEPS approach to leadership or the X-type of leader or administrator.

The Characteristics of a CREEPS Leadership Style (X-type Leader or Administrator)

Control Freak	Makes all the decisions and only engages in a token or superficial effort to seek employee input or suggestions. CREEPS are the ultimate micro-managers. Anything not initiated by the CREEP is rejected.
Relationships with Favorite Employees	Seeks to form relationships with favorite employees; work performance is secondary. Only those in the inner circle of the CREEP are allowed any involvement in the day-to-day managerial activities of the school.
Ego	Has a king- or queen-size ego and views employees as cogs in a machine that can be easily replaced. CREEPS have none or very little concern for employees except for the CREEPS' favorite employees. CREEPS utilize HR policies to intimidate and severely limit employee empowerment.
Limited Ethics	Utilizes a Machiavellian approach to getting tasks accomplished. CREEPS are abusive and manipulative. CREEPS are only concerned about themselves and view others as human pawns who can be used as the CREEP sees fit; any employee development will only occur if it benefits the CREEP.
Power	Loves power and institutes a top-down managerial philosophy. CREEPS are not interested in developing future leaders because those individuals are viewed by CREEPS as threats. CREEPS love to show off their power.
Secretive	Doesn't like to share information with employees. Employees find out information through the grapevine. When a CREEP does have to share information with employees, it's communicated through formal communication channels and generally the employees are not allowed (or only superficially allowed) to be part of the decision-making process.

The difference between the right type of leader (Y-type leader or administrator) and the CREEPS approach (X-type leader or administrator) can also be illustrated by slightly modifying the work of Peters and Austin (1985).

A Description of the Right Type of Leader (Y-type Leader or Administrator)

- Comfortable with people
- Puts employees first

- Open-door cheerleader
- No reserved parking place, private washroom or other facility enhancements such as a larger office, better furniture and so forth
- Common touch
- Good listener
- Fair
- Humble
- Tough, confronts nasty problems
- Tolerant of disagreement (respectful of the opinion of others)
- Has strong convictions (altruistic approach to life)
- Trusts people
- Gives credit, takes blame
- Prefers personal communication over written communication such as memos, email or long reports
- Keeps promises
- Thinks there are at least two other people in the organization who would be good CEOs.

The Description of CREEPS (X-type Leader or Administrator)

- Uncomfortable with people
- Puts their needs first, not the needs of the employees
- Generally inaccessible to employees
- Has a reserved parking place, private washroom and other facility enhancements such as a larger office, better furniture and so forth.
- Strained relationship with employees
- Good talker in terms of outlining what they want, poor listener
- Fair to their favorite employees, exploit the rest
- Arrogant
- Avoid nasty problems, elusive, the artful dodger
- Intolerant of disagreement, does not respect the opinion of others
- No firm stand, vacillates and utilizes a Machiavellian approach
- Distrusts employees and focuses upon numbers on reports
- Takes credit, blames others for failures
- Prefer written communication over personal contact
- Does not keep promises
- Makes sure that no one is hired who remotely resembles a CEO (or a challenge to their authority).

In terms of organizational performance which leadership style will achieve maximum performance? I think it's quite obvious that an organization with the right type of leaders (Y-type leaders or administrators) will outperform an organization filled with CREEPS because the right type of leaders (Y-type leaders or administrators) can tap the full potential of the workforce.

SUMMING IT UP

When it's all said and done, how can we capture the essence of being the right type of leader (Y-type of leader or administrator)? The right type of leadership (Y-type leadership) is always focused upon the right action principle, strives for excellence, keeps procedures, policies, and structure as straight-forward as possible- in other words follows the KISS principle of Keep It Simple Stupid, creates a collaborative workplace- not top-down, and develops the full potential of an organization's most important asset- the employees (managerial and nonmanagerial).

The critical role of leadership can be summarized by the following story that was told by Dr. Ronald Walker (2007) during a doctoral class that I was taking at Jackson State University:

> *You can learn a lot about leadership by watching a farmer trying to get a group of cows to move from one pasture to another. The farmer can get behind the cows and try to push them in the direction he wants the cows to go. Eventually the farmer will get the cows into the next pasture; however, he would have spent a lot of time and used a lot of effort in the process.*
>
> *Instead of trying to push the cows, the farmer could have observed which cow was the lead cow and placed a bucket of feed in front of that cow and easily, with minimum effort, led that cow, and subsequently the other cows, out of one gate and through another into a new pasture. However, what we must always be careful of is who has the bucket and where he is leading us. It could be to the slaughterhouse.*

An Ultimate School Work Environment

- Right Action Priciple: Never Attempt to Achieve Organizational Goals at the Expense of the Employees
- Norm of Reciprocity / Social Exchange Theory
- Efficiency Wage / Merit Pay
- Establish a School Organizational Culture "A" Workplace
- Put Employees First
- The Right Type of Leader: Y-type leader or Administrator

With the right type of leader (Y-type leader or administrator) no one needs to worry about the direction in which the organization is heading for that decision would have been mutually agreed upon between the administration and the employees.

Ultimately it's the values and character of the right type of leader (Y-type leader or administrator) which are grounded within an altruistic approach to life that will allow for the creation of an ultimate school work environment characterized by motivated employees who are always willing to do their best. That's the kind of school that will achieve greatness and be able to sustain an effective learning environment.

REFERENCES

Peters, T. & N. Austin. (1985). *A Passion for Excellence*. New York: Random House

Walker, R. (Spring 2007). Class lecture at Jackson State University.

Chapter Four
Effective Management

In 1961, Harold Koontz summarized the various research approaches that have evolved to address organizational, managerial, and leadership issues. Koontz divided these investigative approaches into six "schools" of thought.

- The first category of scholarship is known as the management process school. Fathered by Henri Fayol, this school of thought examines the functions of management (planning, organizing and staffing, leading, and controlling) in an attempt to improve the management process.
- The empirical school of thought analyzes "real world" cases in the hope of determining what works and what does not in certain situations. Ernest Dale's comparative approach would be an example of this line of inquiry.
- The human behavior school studies how the behavior of individuals impacts organizational outcomes. The premise of this school is that the study of management should focus upon interpersonal relationships since managing involves working with people in order to accomplish certain tasks and organizational goals.
- The social system school utilizes system theory to understand group and organizational performance. Major contributors to this school include Chester Barnard and Herbert Simon.
- The decision theory school can be characterized by its concentration on the decision-making process and the belief that the development of management theory should primarily focus upon analyzing and improving that process.
- The mathematical school views management as a field of study that can be evaluated and improved through the use of mathematical models.

The problem with viewing organizational performance through a particular school of thought is that the analysis becomes too compartmental, or as stated by Gareth Morgan (1997), "a way of seeing is a way of not seeing."

With such a narrow research perspective what has been lacking is the development of a "macro" or comprehensive approach that combines various elements from each school of thought. It's sort of like trying to piece together a jigsaw puzzle without seeing the entire picture of the puzzle on the front of the box. Without the benefit of seeing the whole picture the task of fitting together the pieces of the puzzle becomes more difficult.

By analyzing organizational performance through a comprehensive framework a complete picture can emerge which more fully addresses the many unresolved questions relating to school effectiveness.

A Comprehensive Analysis of Organizational Performance and School Effectiveness

From a macro or comprehensive perspective three primary factors impact school effectiveness: (1) the internal environment of a school, (2) the external environment, and (3) the element of chance that can tilt the level of school effectiveness in a positive or negative direction.

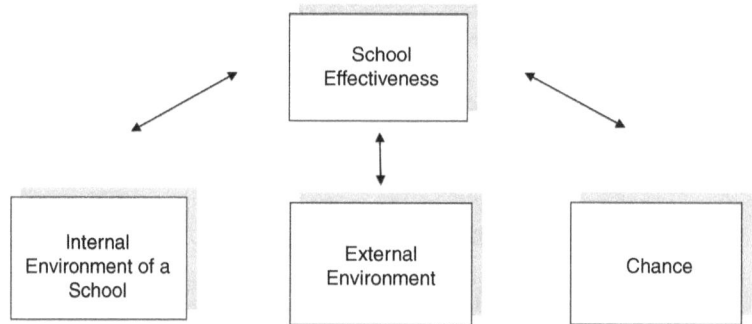

School effectiveness depends upon activities that create an internal environment geared toward achieving a high level of productivity while continually scanning the external environment for conditions that may be favorable to the school in an attempt to reduce the probability that the quality of the learning environment provided by the school will not solely hinge upon the element of chance.

In his groundbreaking book *Future Shock*, Alvin Toffler (1971) described three conditions under which a product can become obsolete. Obsolescence due to function failure occurs when a product physically deteriorates to a point where the product can no longer be utilized. Substantive technological advance refers to a situation where a new, highly competitive product is offered in the marketplace causing another similar product to become obsolete. The third condition that causes a product to become obsolete is when it no longer meets the needs of consumers. Similarly, a school can fall prey to obsolescence, wither, and eventually become an ineffective learning environment.

A School Can Become Obsolete and Eventually Become an Unproductive and Ineffective Learning Environment

When evaluating school effectiveness we cannot ignore the truism that how administrators choose to utilize their authority in the workplace can have tremendous positive or negative implications upon employee performance. For example, according to W. Edwards Deming, long considered the "father of quality control," 85% of all problems in industry could be attributed to "common source of variation" or factors under the control of management and that only 15% resulted from "special causes of variation" or quality problems due to employee/worker errors.

Deming insisted that it is up to management to correct system problems and create a workplace environment that promotes quality and enables workers to achieve their full potential. It's the employees who breathe life into an organization, for it's their skills and abilities that give an organization its competitiveness.

85% of the Problems in Industry are Under the Control of Management

My premise is not to blame the administration for every school failure but to suggest that the time has arrived for a paradigm shift in the relationship between administrators and the employees. Administrators must come to the realization that organizational performance is enhanced when they view employees as partners not subordinates; in other words the administration must put the employees first—and mean it.

The managerial philosophy of putting the employees first and reinforcing that philosophy through the policies and practices established by the administration is one of the features that distinguish an ultimate school work environment from the rest. As for the employees they must continually attempt to increase productivity and strive for excellence in every task they perform as the administration accepts the employees as equal partners.

Specifically, in the educational arena, organizational productivity and positive educational outcomes are achieved through the people of a school.

Changing the Managerial (Administrative)–Employee Relationship Paradigm and Developing an Ultimate School Work Environment

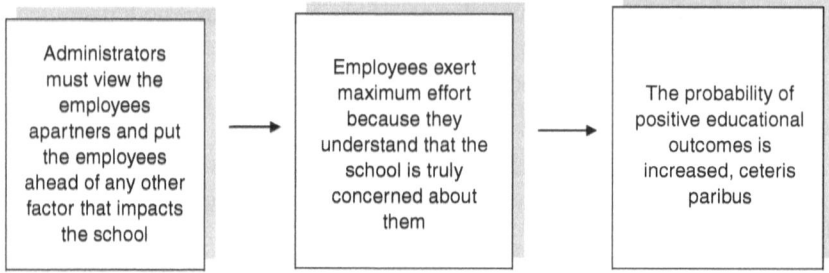

Changing the management–employee paradigm is an important ingredient in developing an ultimate school workplace.

How does your school treat you? Does your school act as if you are its most important asset or just another cost? How does the culture of your school impact your work performance?

After studying management, leadership, organizational behavior, marketing, economics, and educational leadership since the 1980s and working in numerous administrative positions, this author has come to the conclusion that organizations (including schools) that establish policies and practices that clearly demonstrate a true concern for the employees have set the stage where the employees will be more likely to put forth the maximum effort to take care of the priorities of the organization.

Since school outcomes primarily hinge upon the employees (administrative and nonadministrative) what management principles can be utilized to foster an effective and efficient workplace?

Effective Management Principles

- In most situations, a participative management style increases the probability of organizational success. Employees should be viewed as partners, not subordinates.
- The best technique to increase motivation is to create an ultimate school work environment.
- Motivational gimmicks have little to no impact. In fact, motivational gimmicks might have negative consequences upon morale, motivation, and employee commitment to the school.

- Individuals will only change their behavior if they want to and thus it's extremely important to immediately address any personnel issues that have a negative impact on the school.
- An effective administrator is aware of external factors that have a positive or negative impact upon the school.
- The culture of a school (and any subculture) should be driven by a managerial philosophy of "putting the employees first" and empowering the employees as much as possible. Schools that put their employees first will increase the probability of having employees dedicated to providing an effective learning environment because the employees understand that the school truly believes in them and is willing to put the survival of the school on the line when it comes to taking care of the employees.
- Putting employees first involves paying an efficiency wage, rewarding individual, group,* and organizational** level work performance based upon merit, and providing a comprehensive benefits package.
- Putting employees first does not mean that nonperforming employees are not documented and eventually terminated from the school, if necessary. If a nonperforming employee does not improve his or her performance, then he or she must be dismissed. Nonperforming employees are like a cancer that slowly but surely eats away at the effectiveness of the school.
- An effective administrator is guided by the right action principle.

Bringing about a paradigm shift in the administrative-employee relationship will not be easy, for many organizations (including schools) claim to put their employees first, but few do. In terms of improving morale, motivation, productivity, and employee commitment it is the actions of the administration that are what's important, not their words.

Administrative Actions Are Important, Not Words

SUMMING IT UP

Becoming an ultimate school workplace requires having an effective administrative team. Efficient school administrators are guided by the following management principles:

- Craft a school vision and mission statement that is shared and supported by all stakeholders.
- Build the culture of the school around the right action principle and putting employees first.
- Create a safe, efficient, and effective workplace.

- Develop a collaborative relationship with local, state, national, and international educational stakeholders.
- Promote ethical conduct.
- Foster an awareness of the larger cultural, legal, economic, political, and social forces that impact the school.

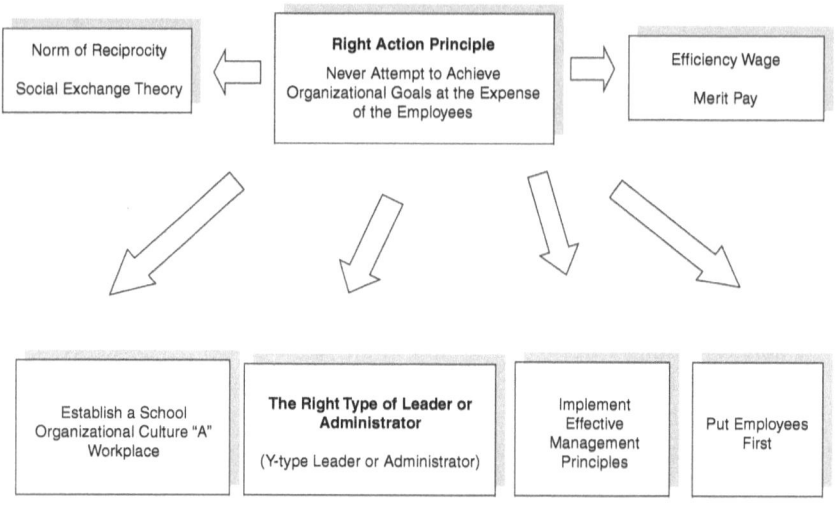

An Ultimate School Work Environment

A REMINDER

* For our purposes, a group refers to academic departments such as the math department or English department and so forth.

** The organizational level refers to the entire school.

REFERENCES

Koontz, H. (December 1961). The Management Theory Jungle. In *Management & Organizational Behavior Classics* (7th Ed.), Matteson, M. & Ivancevich, J. (eds.). Boston, MA: Irwin/McGraw-Hill.

Morgan, G. (1997). *Images of Organization.* Thousand Oaks, CA: Sage Publications, Inc.

Toffler, A. (1971). *Future Shock.* New York: Bantam Books, pp. 68–69.

Chapter Five

Completing the Leadership and Management Picture

Stephen Laws (1987), a horror novelist, once wrote "A man is what his thoughts are every day." Each of us express our thoughts or opinions about everything ranging from a particular coaching decision during a football game to what we think about another person, to the quality or worth of a work of art.

Our opinions or attitudes may or may not be based upon any facts but every attitude has three components. The cognitive component is the intellectual or belief segment of an attitude. The affective component is the feeling or emotional segment of an attitude. The behavioral component is an intention to behave in a certain manner toward someone or something.

The Three Components of Every Attitude

Cognitive Component

Affective Component

Behavioral Component

Important workplace attitudes include: job satisfaction, job involvement, and organizational commitment. An individual with a high level of job satisfaction and job involvement has a positive attitude toward the job and strongly identifies with and cares about the kind of work he does. Individuals with a high level of job satisfaction and job involvement tend to also have a high regard for the organization in terms of loyalty, identification, and organizational involvement.

> **Three Workplace Attitudes**
>
> Job Satisfaction
>
> Job Involvement
>
> Organizational Commitment

A high level of job satisfaction, job involvement, and organizational commitment stems from creating an ultimate school work environment and matching the physical and intellectual abilities of an employee with the job. When trying to match the abilities of an employee to the job, it's critical that we understand the characteristics of the job, and a useful tool for accomplishing that is the job characteristics model (JCM).

The Job Characteristics Model (JCM)

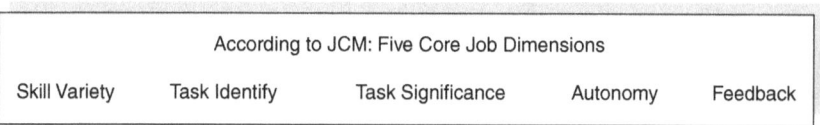

According to the JCM model, every job has five core dimensions: skill variety, task identify, task significance, autonomy, and feedback. Skill variety is the degree to which the job requires a variety of different activities. Task identify is the degree to which the job requires completion of a whole and identifiable piece of work. Task significance is the degree to which the job has a substantial impact on the lives or work of other people. Autonomy is the degree to which the job provides substantial freedom and discretion to the individual in scheduling the work and in determining the procedures to be used in carrying it out. Feedback is the degree to which carrying out the work activities results in the individual obtaining feedback about the effectiveness of his or her performance.

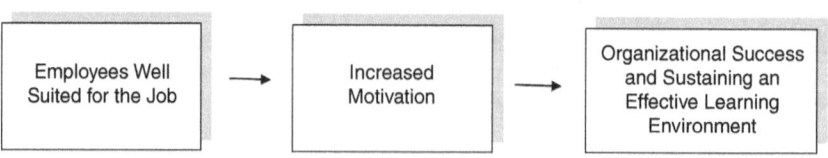

When employees are well suited for the job, remarkable levels of productivity can be achieved. Productive employees are motivated employees. Motivation refers to an individual's willingness to exert high levels of effort. Employees are willing and able to exert a high level of effort when the employee ability–job match is in equilibrium, when recognition is provided for accomplishments and when opportunities for advancement are available for those employees who desire them. A motivated workforce sets the stage for organizational success and sustaining an effective learning environment. Making a "true" commitment to the employees is the signature of an ultimate school work environment and the calling card of the right type of leader (Y-type leader or administrator), and it's the leader's commitment that inspires the employees to want to accomplish organizational goals in the most efficient and effective manner. In other words, the right type of leader (Y-type leader or administrator) can motivate and lead others toward achieving extraordinary organizational results in the short-run and more importantly, in the long-run.

By the way, leadership and management are not the same managerial concepts. I like to think of leadership as doing the right thing while management entails doing the right thing, the right way. Leadership is about providing organizational direction and stimulating high performance among the employees. Management focuses upon the short-term and long-term activities of planning, organizing and staffing, and controlling outcomes.

- Planning is evaluating a situation utilizing the strategic planning process which entails reviewing the strengths and weaknesses of an organization and analyzing the external opportunities and threats (SWOT analysis). The strategic planning process should result in determining the organizational goals that will be pursued and deciding the actions that will be taken to achieve the goals.

In its purest form, strategic planning is all about (1) discovering critical factors in a situation and (2) designing a way of coordinating and focusing actions to deal with those critical factors.

- Organizing and staffing includes assembling the human, physical, financial, and informational resources that are necessary to accomplish organizational tasks in an efficient and effective manner.
- Controlling the workplace involves monitoring organizational workflow and taking corrective action if necessary.

A good manager or administrator is good at these functions; however, that does not mean that a good manager or administrator is a good leader or that a good leader is a good manager or administrator. I am sure that all of us have known an individual who was a good manager or administrator, but not a good leader and vice-versa.

Management and Leadership Are Not the Same Concepts

An ultimate school work environment has great leaders (the right type of leaders—Y-type leaders) and effective administrators (Y-type administrators).

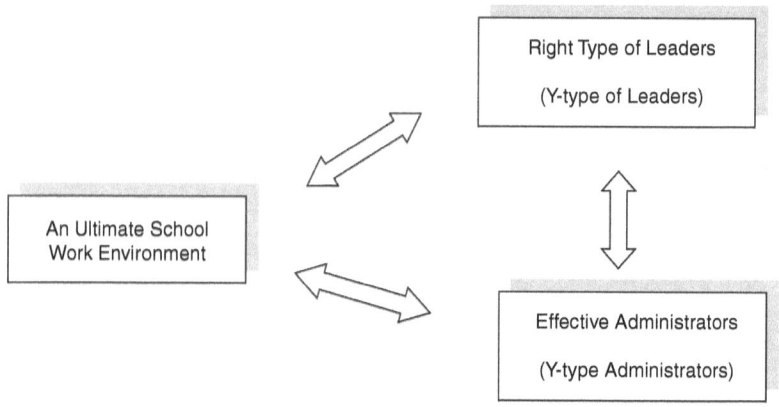

SUMMING IT UP

How can we encapsulate the managerial concepts of leadership, management, and motivation so we do not become lost in all the details?

Both the right type of leader and an effective manager or administrator must be guided by the right action principle; however, a leader's job is to help change context, meaning introducing new elements into the situation that influence behavior for the better (Fullan, 2003, p. 1).

The right type of leader (Y-type leader) fosters a school organizational culture that:

- Strives for excellence.
- Keeps the organizational bureaucracy to a minimum.
- Creates a collaborative workplace, not top-down.
- Develops the full potential of each employee (administrative and nonadministrative).
- Motivates employees to accomplish organizational objectives in an effective and efficient manner.

Completing the Leadership and Management Picture

An effective administrator (Y-type administrator):

- Provides opportunities to achieve high performance.
- Rewards high performance at the individual, group,* and organizational** level.
- Creates procedures, policies, and structure that establish a positive work environment.
- Removes, in an ethical manner, internal and external barriers that interfere with organizational accomplishments.
- Develops control systems to monitor organizational progress.

In the final analysis, a high level of job satisfaction, job involvement, and organizational commitment are a product of combining the right type of leadership (Y-type leader) with effective management principles (Y-type administrator).

From a slightly different view, we can classify an ultimate school work environment and the concepts of job satisfaction, job involvement, and organizational commitment like this:

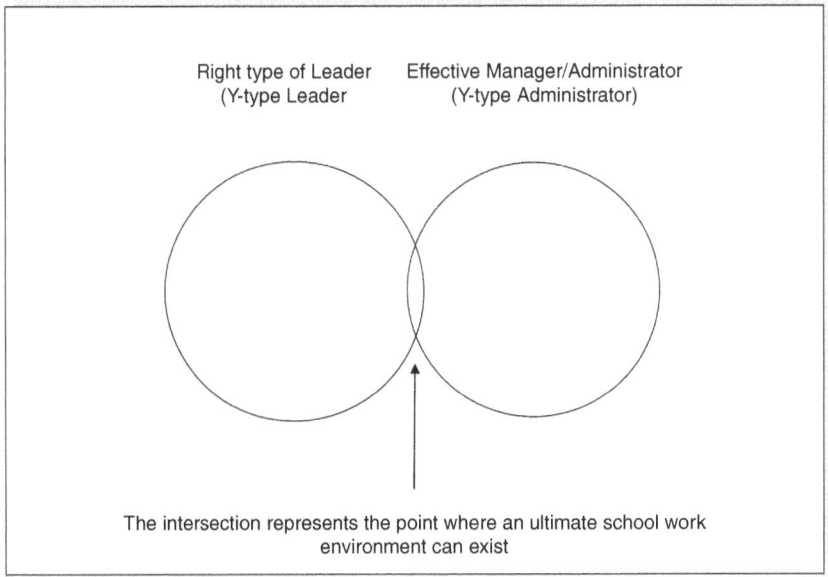

With a high level of job satisfaction, job involvement, and organizational commitment the learning environment will be maximized, ceteris paribus.

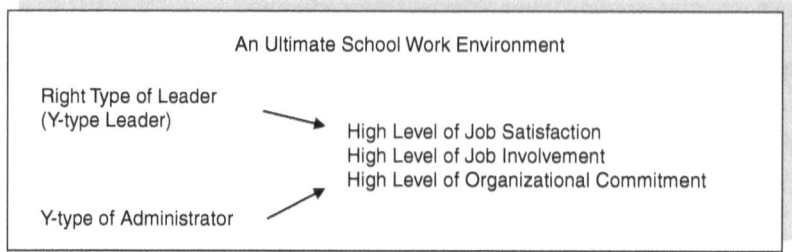

A REMINDER

* For our purposes, a group refers to academic departments such as the math department or English department and so forth.

** The organizational level refers to the entire school.

REFERENCES

Fullan, M. (2003). *The Moral Imperative of School Leadership*. Thousand Oaks, CA: Corwin Press, Inc., p. 1.

Laws, S. (1987). *The Wyrm*. New York: Leisure Books, p. 86.

Part II

MEASURING AN ULTIMATE SCHOOL WORK ENVIRONMENT

A truth insisting on discovery
—Koontz, 2008, p. 95

Chapter Six

What Does an Ultimate School Work Environment Look Like?

Taking care of first things first—to gain a better understanding of organizational performance and how to improve the effectiveness of a school—we must venture deep into the realm of strategic planning, decision making, and value creation.

The role of strategic planning is to keep an organization on track and focused on the activities that it does best so that it does not drift into mediocrity. Strategic planning should improve management decision-making and give the organization a competitive advantage.

> **In the educational arena, a competitive advantage should increase the probability of establishing an ultimate school workplace and sustaining an effective learning environment.**

The hallmarks of strategic planning are analysis, development of a course of action aimed at achieving a competitive advantage, implementation of that course of action, constant feedback, and taking corrective measures when necessary.

The holy grail of the strategic planning process is to learn how to make better managerial decisions, as measured by the competitive advantage that the organization achieves over its rivals from the viewpoint of the organization's stakeholders.

Holy Grail of the Strategic Planning Process

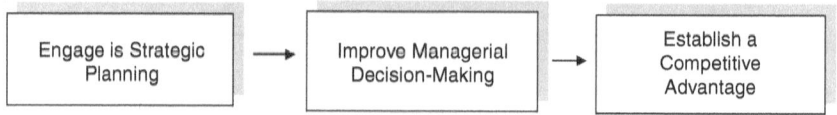

MANAGERIAL DECISION-MAKING

Systems engineering pioneer Andrew Sage describes managerial decision-making as the processes of thought and action involving an irrevocable allocation of resources that culminates in choice behavior. "The quality of a decision depends on how well the decision maker is able to acquire information, to analyze information, and to evaluate and interpret information such as to discriminate between relevant and irrelevant bits of data," Sage wrote in 1981.

Henry Mintzberg (1973) identified four basic roles that managerial decision makers tend to assume in an organization:

- The entrepreneur, who voluntarily initiates change.
- The disturbance handler, who assists in settling disputes.
- The resource allocator, who decides how scarce organizational resources will be distributed.
- The negotiator, who represents the organization in reaching agreements with other organizations.

The quality of the decision is influenced by skills that the manager or administrator possesses. Most successful managers or administrators have a battery of technical, interpersonal, conceptual, and diagnostic skills that they use quite effectively.

- Technical skills are the skills necessary to accomplish specific tasks within the organization.
- Interpersonal skills are the skills that make up the manager's ability to communicate with, understand, and motivate individuals and groups.
- Conceptual skills are the skills that have to do with thinking in the abstract.
- Diagnostic skills are the skills that involve understanding cause-and-effect relationships and recognizing the optimal solutions to a problem.

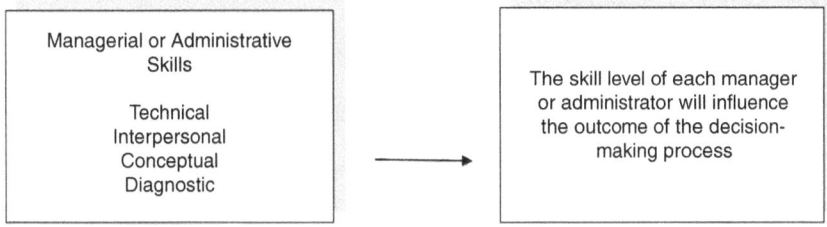

DECISION-MAKING MODELS

Numerous models have been established to illustrate the decision-making process, including the optimizing decision-making model, the so-called satisficing model, the implicit favorite model, organizational procedures view, intuitive model, political view, and individual differences perspective.

> Various Decision-Making Models:
>
> The Optimizing Model
>
> The Satisficing Model
>
> The Implicit Favorite Model
>
> The Organizational Procedures View
>
> The Intuitive Model
>
> The Political View
>
> The Individual Differences Perspective

The first decision-making model, the optimizing model, can be traced back to the "rational manager" view. This is the classic conception of decision making in organizations, developed from the microeconomic notion of a rational, completely informed, single decision maker. In this model of decision making, the decision maker proceeds through six steps that result in the selection of the optimal solution:

Step 1: Ascertain the need for a decision.
Step 2: Identify the decision criteria.

Step 3: Allocate weights to the criteria.
Step 4: Develop the alternatives.
Step 5: Evaluate the alternatives.
Step 6: Select the best alternative.

Lurking behind these steps is the assumption of rationality—the notion that choices are consistent and value maximizing. The decision maker displays several characteristics:

Goal Orientation	The decision maker has a single, well-defined goal that he or she is trying to maximize
Options	The decision maker is fully comprehensive in his or her ability to assess criteria and alternatives
Preferences	Rationality assumes that the criteria and alternatives can be assigned numerical values and ranked in a preferential order
Constancy	The same criteria and alternatives should be obtained every time; the specific decision criteria are constant; and the weights assigned to them are stable over time
Outcome	The final choice will maximize the outcome because the decision maker will select the alternative that rates the highest

The second decision-making model uses the satisficing model and world-renowned economist Herbert Simon's concept of bounded rationality. (Simon coined the term *satisfice*. It is presumed to relate to both *satisfy* and *suffice*.) The general premise of bounded rationality is this, as first explained by Simon: Individuals make decisions by constructing simplified models that extract the essential features from problems without capturing all their complexity. A decision maker selects the first solution that is good enough to solve the issue at hand. In other words, satisficing refers to decision making that seeks an acceptable solution, as opposed to an optimal solution.

A third managerial decision-making model is the implicit favorite model. In this decision-making model, the decision maker selects an alternative early in the decision process, and tends to be less objective about all the other choices.

A fourth decision-making model referred to as the organizational procedures view stems from the work of R. M. Cyert and J. G. March's *A Behavioral Theory of the Firm,* published in 1963. In this theory, the desire to identify organizational roles, channels of communication, and relationships drives decision making. The formal and informal structure of an organization, its standard operating procedures, and its channels of communication are the important variables influencing decision making.

The fifth managerial decision-making model is called the intuitive model. In this model, the decision maker makes a decision based on his or her experience. In this case, the decision-making process and rational analysis work together.

According to a sixth model of decision making (the political view), all decisions are determined as an outcome of power and influence. Power, influence, compromise, and negotiation are among various organizational factors and units that influence a decision.

A final model of managerial decision-making is the individual differences perspective. In this model, the problem-solving and information-processing capabilities of a decision maker are the most important factors influencing the decision-making process. Important in this theory is the concept of cognitive complexity and the "U-curve." The U-curve hypothesis from H. M. Schroder, M. J. Driver, and S. Streufert (1967) implies that a decision maker can only process a certain amount of information, given a certain environmental complexity (up to a maximum point), after which the information processing of a decision maker is diminished.

In summary, decision-making models provide a framework for focusing a decision maker's attention on creating a competitive advantage.

ANOTHER STRATEGIC PLANNING PERSPECTIVE

In 1980, Derek F. Abell proposed that the framework of the strategic planning process could be built on the answers to three critical questions:

Who is being satisfied?
What is being satisfied?
How are the needs of the customers being satisfied?

If you determine who is being satisfied, you can identify the customer base (or target market). The other two questions focus attention on the needs of the target market, and how an organization can best meet those needs. In essence, the three questions proposed by Abell form the basis by which organizational decision makers identify or define the purpose of the organization.

Thus, the strategic planning process is utilized to systematically address the questions proposed by Abell. The strategic planning process consists of five basic steps that can be followed simultaneously.

> **Define the Purpose of an Organization by Three Questions**
>
> Who is Being Satisfied?
>
> What is Being Satisfied?
>
> How are the Needs of the Customer Being Satisfied?

Step 1: Formulate the corporate mission and vision statements, and identify the major organizational goals.

Step 2: Analyze the organization's external competitive environment to identify opportunities and threats.

Step 3: Analyze the organization's internal operating environment to identify the organization's strengths and weaknesses.

Step 4: Select strategies that build on the organization's strengths and correct its weaknesses to take advantage of external opportunities and counter external threats.

Step 5: Implement strategy. Design appropriate organizational structures and control systems to put the organization's chosen strategy into action.

If we look at strategic planning from a different angle, we see that the process can be separated into two dimensions: strategy and operational effectiveness. Michael Porter, a business professor at Harvard University (and probably the leading authority on strategic planning), believes that strategy is a plan for competing in the marketplace, whereas operational effectiveness is the ability to perform operational tasks more efficiently than competitors. The end product of the strategic planning process is to always establish a competitive advantage.

COMPETITIVE ADVANTAGE

Some experts contend that competitive advantage is really a strategy to give an organization a distinct advantage over its competition. According to Michael Porter in his 1985 work *Competitive Advantage,* an organization must select a competitive strategy in order to successfully perform at an above-average profitability level because no firm can be all things to all people. Porter proposed three competitive strategy options: cost leadership, a differentiation strategy, and a focus strategy.

Cost leadership is a strategy in which an organization attempts to be the lowest-cost producer in its industry. A firm can obtain a low-cost advantage through efficient operations, economies of scale, technological innovation, low-cost labor, or preferential access to raw materials.

A differentiation strategy occurs when an organization attempts to distinguish itself from its industry competitors within a broad market. To achieve a differentiation strategy, an organization strives to obtain a unique position in the marketplace by emphasizing high quality, extraordinary service, an innovative product design, technological capability, or an unusually positive brand image. The key is that the unique position that the organization is attempting to establish must be significantly different from its rivals to justify a price premium that exceeds the cost of differentiating.

A focus strategy is when an organization wants to establish an advantage in a narrow market segment. The focus strategy utilizes either a cost advantage or a differentiation approach aimed at a narrow market segment.

In order to achieve long-term success, an organization must sustain its competitive advantage. Tactics that organizations use to achieve a long-run competitive advantage include establishing barriers to entry, such as patents, copyrights, trademarks, or economies of scale. Organizations sometimes lower prices to gain market share, tie up suppliers with exclusive contracts, or lobby Congress to impose trade restrictions designed to limit foreign competition.

Underlying Porter's three competitive strategies are the generic building blocks of competitive advantage, as described by Charles W. L. Hill and Gareth R. Jones (1998):

1. Superior efficiency is about converting inputs into outputs. Inputs are the basic factors of production, such as labor, land, capital, management, and technological know-how. Outputs are the goods and services that an organization produces. The more efficiently an organization can convert inputs into outputs, the higher the productivity level of that organization. The organization with the highest level of productivity in an industry typically has the lowest costs of production, and therefore gains a competitive advantage.
2. The impact of superior product quality on competitive advantage is twofold. First, providing high-quality products increases the value of those products in the eyes of the consumer (target market) that allows the organization to charge a higher price. The second impact of high quality on competitive advantage comes from the greater efficiency and lower unit cost it brings.
3. Superior innovation is the most important of the building blocks of competitive advantage. Innovation can be defined as anything new or novel

about the way an organization operates or about the products it produces. Innovative organizations provide consumers with products that are not available from other firms. That lack of availability allows the organization to charge a premium for its product. In addition, innovative organizations can build brand loyalty, which makes it more difficult for rivals to gain market share.
4. Superior customer service or responsiveness is achieved by identifying and satisfying the needs of the consumers (target market) better than any other organization. Superior customer responsiveness includes such activities as quality, customization, response time, design, and superior service before and after the sale.

Organizations that focus on the building blocks of competitive advantage increase the probability of improving the organization's performance. When everything else is said and done, increasing the performance of an organization is what leadership and management is all about!

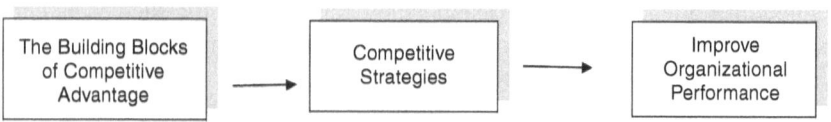

OUTPUT VALUE CREATION AND COMPETITIVE ADVANTAGE

Another important concept connected with the building blocks of competitive advantage is the notion of output value creation—the value of the product or service produced by an organization.

An organization creates output value by developing a strategic plan that focuses on the building blocks of competitive advantage. This plan should address the needs of the target market and the employees. In this context, the target market will be specifically referred to as a group of people for which an organization designs, implements, and maintains a strategic plan intended to meet the needs of that target market, resulting in mutually satisfying exchanges.

The output value generated by an organization is measured by the equation $V = B/P$ (the letter V represents value; B represents perceived and/or actual benefits; and P represents the price of the product). A higher output value as perceived by the target market increases the probability of organizational sustainability.

VALUE CREATION, THE IMPORTANCE OF THE EMPLOYEES, AND CREATING AN ULTIMATE SCHOOL WORK ENVIRONMENT

Lurking beneath the equation V = B/P is the ability of the workforce and individual employees to create product benefits in an efficient manner. Thus, the lesson to be learned is that employee performance drives the value creation process, and in the educational arena, the key to unlocking employee performance is establishing an ultimate school work environment.

Given the critical link between the elements of an ultimate school work environment and the value creation process, how do we describe an ultimate school workplace? First, an ultimate school work environment is not Camelot, for Camelot is a mystical place that only exists in mankind's collective imagination. In Camelot, all wrongs are righted, all injustices are corrected, and evil in any form is eventually overcome by the power of goodness.

An Ultimate School Work Environment and Value Creation

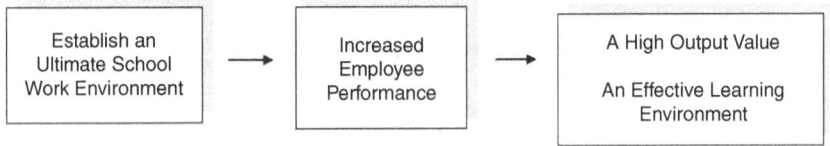

So if not Camelot, what is an ultimate school work environment? Simply put, a school that is an ultimate school work environment has the following features:

- Adequate and fair compensation for all employees (administrative and nonadministrative) based upon merit performance at the individual, group,* and organizational** level. This includes protection against being laid off or terminated.
- A safe, healthy, comfortable and attractive workplace that is equipped with adequate resources to perform the required job tasks.
- Challenging and mutually agreed upon goals at the individual, group,* and organizational** level. This includes clearly stated rules and expectations as well as a clear chain of command. Jobs that develop human capacities and provide a chance for personal growth and financial security.
- A social environment that accepts and promotes each employee's personal identity and characteristics (within reasonable behavior and ethical limits).
- A workplace free from prejudice and based upon merit.

- A school culture based upon a sense of community, upward mobility, and constitutionalism (the rights of personal privacy, dissent, and due process).
- A work role that minimizes infringement on personal leisure time and family needs outside of normal work hours.
- Socially responsible organizational actions.
- Job autonomy meaning working without close supervision and being free to make decisions about one's job independently.
- Control over the work process including the pace, schedule, the demands of the job, and acquisition of new knowledge, skills, and (or) abilities.
- Opportunities to work and interact with other personnel and departments as well as being able to help others improve their job performance.

Educational decision makers who decide to move beyond the traditional, normal school approach and build an ultimate school work environment will be among the few willing to travel down that road, but for those willing to do so, the positive learning outcomes are limitless.

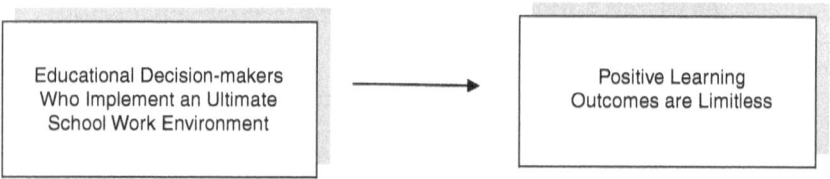

SUMMING IT UP

At its basic level, high performance essentially revolves around knowing how the abilities of each employee differ, and using that knowledge to increase the likelihood that any employee will consistently perform his or her job well.

Employee job performance begins the "chain" of workplace activity that determines the level of productivity that a group* or organization** will eventually achieve. Productive environments at the group* or organizational** level are linked to and depend on the performance of each employee. Like any link in a chain, the productivity that a group* or organization** can achieve will only be as high as the weakest link in the chain of workplace activity. Group* accomplishments and organizational** productivity are a function of individual accomplishments and productivity.

Chain of Workplace Activity

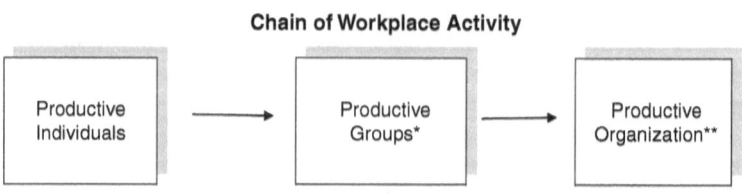

Generally, how well an employee performs on the job will be reflective of the employee's intellectual and physical abilities, as well as the job fit between an employee's abilities and the job task.

Intellectual ability refers to an employee's capability to do mental activities. The seven most frequently cited dimensions making up intellectual abilities are listed below:

1. Number aptitude is the ability to do speedy and accurate arithmetic.
2. Verbal comprehension is the ability to understand what is read or heard and the relationship between the words.
3. Perceptual speed is the ability to identify visual similarities and differences quickly and accurately.
4. Inductive reasoning is the ability to identify a logical sequence in a problem, and then to solve the problem.
5. Deductive reasoning is the ability to use logic and assess the implications of an argument.
6. Spatial visualization is the ability to imagine how an object would look if its position in space were changed.
7. Memory is the ability to retain and recall past experiences.

Physical ability refers to the stamina, dexterity, strength, and similar characteristics that are required to perform a task. The nine basic abilities involved in the performance of physical tasks are listed below:

1. Dynamic strength is the ability to exert muscular force repeatedly or continuously over time.
2. Trunk strength is the ability to exert muscular strength using the trunk (particularly abdominal) muscles.
3. Static strength is the ability to exert force against external objects.
4. Explosive strength is the ability to expend a maximum of energy in one or a series of explosive acts.
5. Extent flexibility is the ability to move the trunk and back muscles as far as possible.
6. Dynamic flexibility is the ability to make rapid, repeated flexing movements.
7. Body coordination is the ability to coordinate the simultaneous actions of different parts of the body.
8. Balance is the ability to maintain equilibrium, despite forces pulling off-balance.
9. Stamina is the ability to continue maximum effort when prolonged effort is required over time.

To maximize employee performance, you must match the intellectual and physical abilities of an employee to the job. When the employee ability–job match is out of equilibrium because the employee's abilities exceed or are not sufficient to perform the task, the performance level of the employee will be marginal, at best. Marginally performing employees result in underperforming groups* and an unproductive, noncompetitive organization.**

The Employee Ability–Job Match is out of Equilibrium

| Mismatch Between Employee Abilities and the Job | → | Low Employee Productivity | → | Underperforming Groups* | → | A Lower Output Value Created by the Organization** |

On the other hand, when the employee ability–job match is in equilibrium, an unproductive workplace can be transformed into a productive environment that generates a high output value. This transformation requires a commitment to building an ultimate school work environment. Within this type of work environment, employee productivity is nourished and strengthened. As employee productivity gains strength and expands, output value increases; just like the trunk and branches of a tree stretch further and further toward the sky when its roots are firmly planted in fertile ground.

Given the importance of an ultimate school work environment, how do we know when one exists? Here is how Thompson and Stickland (2003) put it:

> Organizations with a spirit of high performance typically are intensely people-oriented, and they reinforce their concern for individual employees on every conceivable occasion in every conceivable way. They treat employees with dignity and respect, train each employee thoroughly, encourage employees to use their own initiative and creativity in performing their work, set reasonable and clear performance standards, hold managers at every level responsible for developing the people who report to them, and grant employees enough autonomy to stand out, excel, and contribute. Creating a results-oriented organizational culture generally entails making champions out of the people who turn in winning performances.

The bottom line is that an ultimate school work environment supports such a high quality of work life that those individuals who work there never want to leave for they can find no better place to work and as a result are always motivated to put forth the maximum effort to achieve organizational goals.

What Does an Ultimate School Work Environment Look Like?

An Ultimate School Work Environment—Individual, Group*, and Organizational Success**

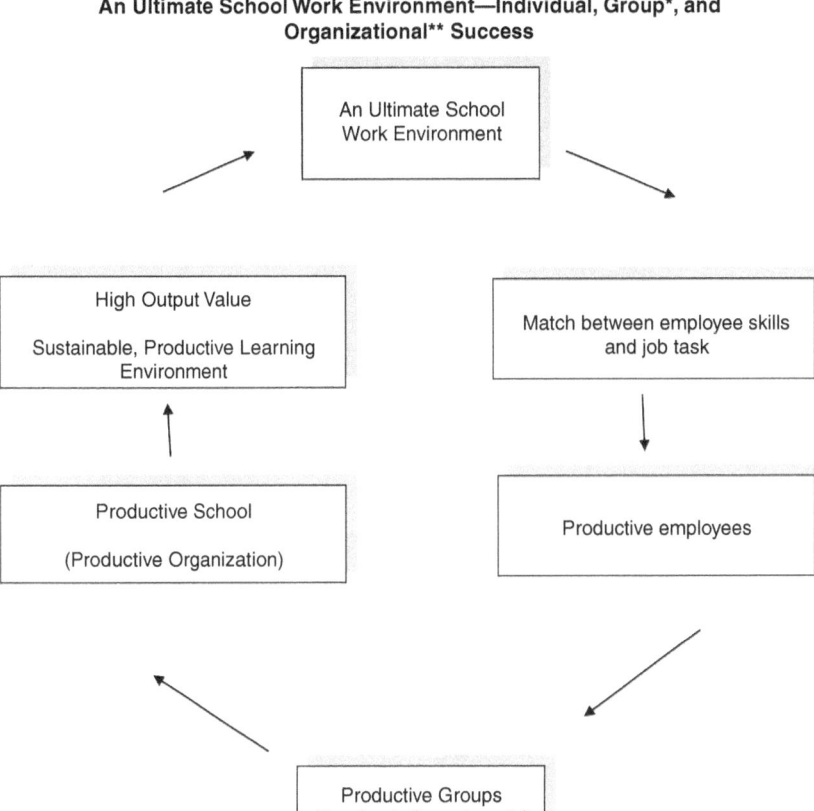

A REMINDER

* A group refers to academic departments such as the math department or English department and so forth
** Organizational level refers to the entire school

REFERENCES

Abell, D. (1980). *Defining the business: The starting point of strategic planning.* Englewood Cliffs, NJ: Prentice Hall.
Hill, C. W. L. & G. R. Jones. (1998). *Strategic Management: An Integrated Approach.* Boston, MA: Houghton Mifflin.
Koontz, D. (2008). *Your heart belongs to me.* NY: Bantam, p. 95
Mintzberg, H. (1973). *The Nature of Managerial Work.* New York: Harper and Row.

Porter, M. (1985). *Competitive Advantage: Creating and Sustaining Superior Performance.* New York: The Free Press.

Sage, A. (September 1981). Behavioral and organizational considerations in the design of information systems and processes for planning and decision support, IEEE Transactions on Systems, Man, and Cybernetics, SMC-11, 9, 640–678.

Schroder, H., Driver, M., & Steufert, S. (1967). Human information processing. NY: Holt, Rinehart, & Winston, Inc.

Thompson, A. & A. J. Stickland III. (2003). *Strategic Management: Concepts and Cases.* New York: McGraw-Hill Irwin.

Chapter Seven

Does Your School Measure Up?

In the previous chapter, we learned that establishing an ultimate school work environment creates a situation where productivity can thrive and the output value-creation process can flourish, just like a long-overdue rain can transform a barren patch of land into a garden oasis.

Gaining an understanding of the value-creation process was a vital step forward in our understanding of the importance of an ultimate school workplace. However, our final destination involves moving beyond the value-creation process for we must discover a measurement tool that can quantify whether a school is an ultimate school workplace.

So like a group of explorers we must continue to push ahead in our quest to unlock the characteristics of an ultimate school work environment. However, sometimes to move forward one needs to look back at what has already been uncovered. It is peculiar but true that when one is searching for something or unsure of a particular course of action, the best approach for determining what to do is often to examine what has already taken place in the past. Then the path to the future becomes clear. So here's what we know so far about an ultimate school work environment:

- Everything regarding an ultimate school work environment begins with the right action principle.
- In an ultimate school work environment a norm of reciprocity exists between the school and its employees (administrative and nonadministrative). As a consequence, the principles embedded within social exchange theory are quite evident within an ultimate school work environment.
- Efficient wages are paid and adequate, and fair benefits are provided with the goal of achieving financial security for all employees (administrative and nonadministrative).

- The work environment is free from prejudice, and a truly functioning merit pay system is in place at the individual, group,* and organizational level.**
- A school organizational culture "A" workplace exists.
- "Putting employees first" philosophy is incorporated in the school policies, practices, and procedures.
- The right type of leaders (Y-type leaders and administrators) are in positions of authority throughout the school; there is no place for CREEPS.
- Effective management principles are followed.
- A safe, healthy, comfortable, well-equipped, and attractive workplace exists.
- Challenging and mutually agreed upon goals at the individual, group,* and organizational level** are established. This includes clearly stated rules and expectations as well as a clear chain of command.
- Jobs are designed to develop human capacities meaning that knowledge, skills, and abilities are being enhanced in order to provide a chance for personal growth and greater financial opportunities.
- A social environment is established that accepts and promotes each employee's personal identity and characteristics (within reasonable behavior and ethical limits).
- The school culture is based upon a sense of community, upward mobility, and constitutionalism (the rights of personal privacy, dissent, and due process).
- Job tasks minimize infringement on personal leisure time and family needs outside of normal work hours.
- The school engages in socially responsible actions.
- Job autonomy is encouraged within reasonable limits (meaning working without close supervision and being free to make decisions about one's job independently).
- Employee control over the work process (including the pace, setting one's own schedule, the demands of the job, and acquiring new knowledge, skills, and abilities) is fostered within reasonable limits.
- Opportunities to work and interact with other personnel and departments as well as being able to help others improve their job performance is part of the school culture.

Given the above characteristics, we can now qualify whether a school is an ultimate school work environment.

Is Your School an Ultimate School Work Environment?
Measurement Form

Variables	Points for Variable	Does the school have the variable (Yes or No)	School Points
Is your school governed by the right action principle	2 for yes 0 for no		
Efficient wages are paid and adequate and fair benefits are provided with the goal of achieving financial security for all employees (administrative and non-administrative)	1 for yes 0 for no		
The work environment is free from prejudice and a truly functioning merit pay system is in place at the individual, group, and organizational level	1 for yes 0 for no		
A school organizational culture "A" workplace exists	1 for yes 0 for no		
"Putting employees first" philosophy is incorporated in the school policies, practices, and procedures	1 for yes 0 for no		
The right type of leaders (Y-type leaders and administrators) are in positions of authority through-out your school; there is no place for CREEPS	1 for yes 0 for no		
Effective management principles are followed	1 for yes 0 for no		
A safe, healthy, comfortable, well-equipped, and attractive workplace exists	1 for yes 0 for no		
Challenging and mutually agreed upon goals at the individual, group, and organizational level are established. This includes clearly stated rules and expectations as well as a clear chain of command.	1 for yes 0 for no		
Jobs are designed to develop human capacities (meaning that knowledge, skills, and abilities are being enhanced in order to provide a chance for personal growth and greater financial opportunities)	1 for yes 0 for no		

Is Your School an Ultimate School Work Environment?
Measurement Form

Variables	Points for Variable	Does the school have the variable (Yes or No)	School Points
A social environment is established that accepts and promotes each employees personal identity and characteristics (within reasonable behavioral and ethical limits)	1 for yes 0 for no		
The school culture is based upon a sense of community, upward mobility, and constitutionalism (the rights of personal privacy, dissent, and due process)	1 for yes 0 for no		
Job tasks minimize infringement on personal leisure time and family needs outside of normal work hours	1 for yes 0 for no		
The school engages in socially responsible actions	1 for yes 0 for no		
Job autonomy is encouraged within reasonable limits (meaning working without close supervision and being free to make decisions about one's job independently)	1 for yes 0 for no		
Employee control over the work process (including the pace, setting one's own schedule, the demands of the job, and acquiring new knowledge, skills, and abilities) is fostered within reasonable limits	1 for yes 0 for no		
Opportunities to work and interact with other personnel and departments as well as being able to help others improve their job performance is part of the school culture	1 for yes 0 for no		

A school is an ultimate school work environment if it scores between 16 and 18 points. A school can be classified as a normal school approach plus (+) if its score is between 14 and 15 points. If the school score is between 12 and 13 points, then that workplace can be labeled as a normal school approach minus (−). A below normal school approach would be a score of

Does Your School Measure Up?

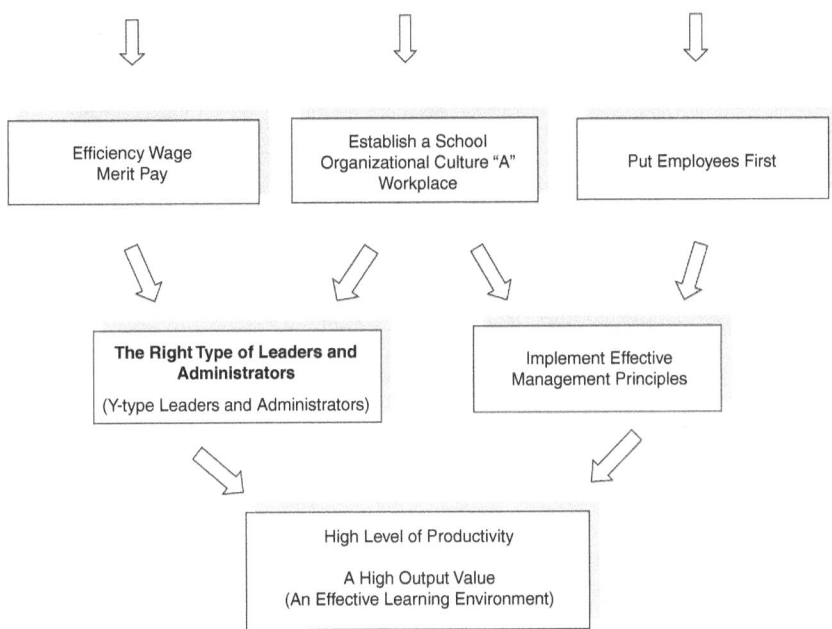

between 10 and 11 points. A school that scores 9 points or below can be identified as a let's get out of here as soon as possible school.

SUMMING IT UP

Achieving our final destiny of discovering a measurement tool that captures the essence of an ultimate school work environment began by unlocking the elements of an ultimate school workplace. Our adventure moved forward by revealing a set of characteristics or variables that described an ultimate school work environment and ended by determining how a school measures up to those variables.

Another methodology for portraying whether a school is an ultimate school work environment is summarized below.

An Ultimate School Work Environment (18 to 16 points)

A Normal School Approach Plus (+) (15 to 14 points)

A Normal School Approach Minus (–) (13 to 12 points)

Below Normal School Approach (11 to 10 points)

Let's Get Out of Here as Soon as Possible School (9 or less points)

A REMINDER

* For our purposes, a group refers to academic departments such as the math department or English department and so forth.

** The organizational level refers to the entire school.

Chapter Eight

Decision Time

Let's review a few statements from the book.

Preface
- Greatness requires great achievements, and the issue becomes how can greatness be best achieved: the Normal School approach or the ultimate school work environment approach?

Introduction
- Have you ever worked for an organization where it felt like no one cared about you and that your contribution to the organization was always minimized or worse, unappreciated?

Chapter 1
- The critical question is what type of organizational culture or work environment will best support an effective learning environment? The answer is an ultimate school work environment.
- The remaining issue is how does a school craft an ultimate school work environment?

Chapter 2
- Three critical workplace parameters are (1) managerial attitudes and practices in the workplace, (2) the organizational environment, and (3) the tasks being performed within an organization. The workplace parameters form the foundation of the Organizational Culture Educational Status Model (OCESM).

64   *Chapter Eight*

- The OCESM establishes a framework to evaluate the culture of a school and provides a methodology for improving the learning environment of a school.
- At the core of the three workplace parameters and the OCESM is the quality of the employees (administrative and nonadministrative) of a school. Failing to recognize this fact puts the effectiveness of the learning environment in serious jeopardy.

Chapter 3
- Which boss would you prefer—the right type of leader (Y-type leader or administrator) or a CREEP (X-type leader or administrator)?
- The right type of leader or administrator can only emerge from an altruistic approach to life.
- The right type of leader or administrator focuses upon the needs of the employees thereby creating a workplace characterized by highly motivated and productive employees who are focused upon establishing an effective learning environment. In other words, the right type of leader or administrator pursues organizational goals and objectives in such a way that the growth and integrity of people are respected.
- Other characteristics of the right type of leader or administrator include: comfortable with people; puts employees first; open-door cheerleader; no reserved parking place or special facility accommodations; common touch; good listener; fair; humble; tough, confronts nasty problems; tolerant of disagreement (respectful of the opinion of others); has strong convictions (altruistic approach to life); trusts people; gives credit, takes blame; prefers personal communication over written communication such as memos, email, or long reports; keeps promises; and thinks there are at least two other people in the organization who would be good administrators.
- CREEPS (X-type leaders or administrators) must always be eliminated from any leadership or administrative position.

Chapter 4
- My premise is not to blame management for every organizational failure but to suggest that the time has arrived for a paradigm shift in the relationship between administration and the employees. Administrators must come to the realization that school performance is enhanced when they view employees as partners not subordinates; in other words administrators must put the employees first—and mean it.
- The managerial philosophy of putting the employees first and reinforcing that philosophy through the policies and practices established by administrators is one of the features that distinguish an ultimate school

work environment from the rest. Administration retains the final decision-making authority, but the focus should be upon how an organizational decision impacts the employees for that in turn will influence how the employees perform their job and ultimately how effective the learning environment will be.
- After studying management, leadership, organizational behavior, marketing, and economics since the 1980s and working in numerous administrative positions, this author has come to the conclusion that schools that establish policies and practices that clearly demonstrate a true concern for the employees have set the stage where the employees will be more likely to put forth the maximum effort to create an effective learning environment.
- Efficient management principles include: (1) craft a school vision and mission that is shared and supported by all stakeholders; (2) build the culture of the school around the right action principle and putting employees first; (3) create a safe, efficient, and effective workplace; (4) develop a collaborative relationship with all stakeholders; (5) promote ethical conduct; and (6) foster an awareness of the larger cultural, legal, economic, political, and social forces that impact the school.

Chapter 5
- A high level of job satisfaction, job involvement, and organizational commitment stems from creating an ultimate school work environment and matching the physical and intellectual abilities of an employee with the job.
- When employees are well suited for the job remarkable levels of productivity can be achieved. Productive employees are motivated employees. Motivation refers to an individual's willingness to exert high levels of effort. Employees are willing and able to exert a high level of effort when the employee ability—job match is in equilibrium, when recognition is provided for accomplishments, and when opportunities for advancement are available for those employees who desire that.
- A motivated workforce sets the stage for sustaining an effective learning environment.
- Motivation is about providing individuals with an opportunity to improve their knowledge, skills, and abilities.

Chapter 6
- The role of strategic planning is to keep the school on track and focused on the activities that enhance the learning environment so that it does not drift into mediocrity.
- To accomplish its role, the strategic planning process should always be the same: (1) discover the critical factors in a situation and (2) design a way of coordinating and focusing actions to deal with those factors.

- Systems engineering pioneer Andrew Sage describes managerial decision-making as the processes of thought and action involving an irrevocable allocation of resources that culminates in choice behavior. The quality of a decision depends on how well the decision maker is able to acquire and evaluate information.
- Schools that focus on the building blocks of competitive advantage increase the probability of improving the effectiveness of the learning environment.
- Another important concept connected with the building blocks of competitive advantage is the notion of value creation—the value of the product or service produced by an organization.
- Lurking beneath the equation $V = B/P$ is the ability of the workforce and individual employees to create an effective learning environment. Thus, the lesson to be learned is that employee performance drives the value creation process and the key to unlocking employee performance is establishing an ultimate school work environment.
- At its basic level, high performance essentially revolves around knowing how the abilities of each employee differ, and using that knowledge to increase the likelihood that any employee will consistently perform his or her job well. Employee job performance begins the "chain" of workplace activity that determines the level of productivity that a group* or organization** will eventually achieve.
- Productive environments at the group* or organizational** level are linked to and depend on the performance of each employee. Like any link in a chain, the productivity that a group* or organization** can achieve can only be as high as the weakest link in the chain of workplace activity. Group* accomplishments and organizational** productivity are a function of individual accomplishments and productivity.
- To maximize individual accomplishments and productivity, you must match the intellectual and physical abilities of an employee to the job.

Chapter 7
- Here's what we know about an ultimate school work environment:
    - Everything regarding an ultimate school work environment begins with the right action principle.
    - In an ultimate school work environment a norm of reciprocity situation exists between the school and its employees (administrative and nonadministrative). As a consequence, the principles embedded within social exchange theory are quite evident within an ultimate school work environment.
    - Efficient wages are paid and adequate and fair benefits are provided with the goal of achieving financial security for all employees (administrative and nonadministrative).

- The workplace is free from prejudice and a truly functioning merit pay system is in place at the individual, group,* and organizational** level.
- A school organizational culture "A" workplace exists.
- "Putting employees first" philosophy is incorporated in the school policies, practices, and procedures.
- The right type of leaders and administrators (Y-type leaders and administrators) are in positions of authority throughout the school; there is no place for CREEPS.
- Effective management principles are followed.
- A safe, healthy, comfortable, well-equipped, and attractive workplace exists.
- Challenging and mutually agreed upon goals at the individual, group,* and organizational** level are established. This includes clearly stated rules and expectations as well as a clear chain of command.
- Jobs are designed to develop human capacities meaning that knowledge, skills, and abilities are being enhanced in order to provide a chance for personal growth and greater financial opportunities.
- A social environment is established that accepts and promotes each employees personal identity and characteristics (within reasonable behavior and ethical limits).
- The school culture is based upon a sense of community, upward mobility, and constitutionalism (the rights of personal privacy, dissent, and due process).
- Job tasks minimize infringement on personal leisure time and family needs outside of normal work hours.
- The school engages in socially responsible actions.
- Job autonomy is encouraged within reasonable limits (meaning working without close supervision and being free to make decisions about one's job independently).
- Employee control over the work process (including the pace, setting one's own schedule, the demands of the job, and acquiring new knowledge, skills, and abilities) is fostered within reasonable limits.
- Opportunities to work and interact with other personnel and departments as well as being able to help others improve their job performance is part of the school or school district culture.

- According to the "Is Your School an Ultimate School Work Environment Measurement Form," a school is an ultimate school work environment if it scores between 16 and 18 points. A school can be classified as a Normal School Approach Plus (+) if its score is between 14 and 15 points. If a school's score is between 12 and 13 points then that workplace can be labeled as a Normal School Approach Minus (–). A "Below Normal School Approach" would be a score of between 10 and 11 points. A school that scores 9 points or less can be identified as a "Let's get out of here as soon as possible school."

Given these statements, shouldn't we all be wondering why school administrators and other educational decision makers tend to resist implementing much of the information contained in this book? Wouldn't a school that is an ultimate school work environment be more productive and be in a better position to sustain an effective learning environment?

The answer to the second question is obvious. As for the first question, it is decision time for administrators and other educational officials, a normal school approach or an ultimate school work environment approach?

SUMMING IT UP

Life and Self-Discovery

As I looked into the night sky, I wanted to reach up and touch the stars. But as I raised my hands towards the heavens, I knew that the sparkling objects seemingly adrift in the calm, dark waters of a faraway ocean were many light years away.

How far does the universe extend? What are its boundaries? Does the universe have any boundaries? As these questions fueled my imagination, I suddenly felt as if mankind was being drawn back to the days of Columbus, who, standing upon the shores of the mighty Atlantic, dreamed of discovering a New World. A world that would forever establish the boundaries of the Earth—like a painting set within its frame.

With my thoughts still drifting among the stars, I wondered what new adventures await our species; what new mysteries would mankind uncover? But most of all I was trying to visualize how our lives would change as we continue to unlock what was once unknown.

The unknown, the gray area of life, offers so many mysteries, the most haunting of which is the quest to uncover the meaning of life. Does life have a purpose? Is there a natural order to the universe? Is there a universal plan? Can the answers to these questions be found in some faraway location in the universe? Do the stars that dot the heavenly landscape mark the trail to that location, like glimmering points on a celestial map, or will mankind be destined to roam upon many paths that never quite lead us to the answers we so desperately seek?

As these thoughts completely engulfed my consciousness, like a thick fog rolling across a field swallowing up everything in sight, the glowing light of the sun began to slowly appear near the horizon, and soon the darkness gave way to the birth of a new day. As the soothing rays of the rising sun gently reached out and touched my face, I suddenly realized that the meaning of life is not found by searching through some remote corner of the universe but will only be revealed through an exploration of the soul. Life is about what we think, what we believe in, how we live our daily life, and most important, how we treat others.

Life is a voyage of self-discovery, and the heavenly light of the stars seem to possess an almost mystical ability to inspire each of us to search deep within our souls and probe for the answers that explain why we are the way we are. This is an intensive, private inquiry that will eventually unmask our "real" identity as every layer of our "outer being" gets peeled away until our "inner being" lies totally exposed. Only after such a journey will our mind and heart be opened to the realization of how we either positively or negatively influence the environment around us.

At the heart of our quest to discover what constitutes an ultimate school work environment is the notion of how we interact with others, for it is the quality of that interaction that distinguishes an ultimate school work environment from other schools. The bottom line is that it is our attitudes and actions which ultimately determine whether an ultimate school work environment can exist.

In *Just After Sunset* Stephen King wrote, "No, he had to decide where the road was, and where it was going." School administrators and other educational decision makers must decide if they want to establish an ultimate school work environment. Positive educational outcomes will spring forth for those school administrators willing to follow the path we travelled in this book.

It's decision time!

A REMINDER

* For our purposes, a group refers to academic departments such as the math department or English department and so forth.

** The organizational level refers to the entire school.

REFERENCE

King, S. (2008). *Just After Sunset.* New York: Pocket Books, p. 18

Conclusion
Final Comment

In the end, it is not about you (the leader or administrator); it is about the people who work for you. This workplace philosophy is embedded within the right action principle.

If your school is guided by the right action principle, your school is probably an ultimate school work environment which means your school is productive, generating a high output value, and outperforming other schools.

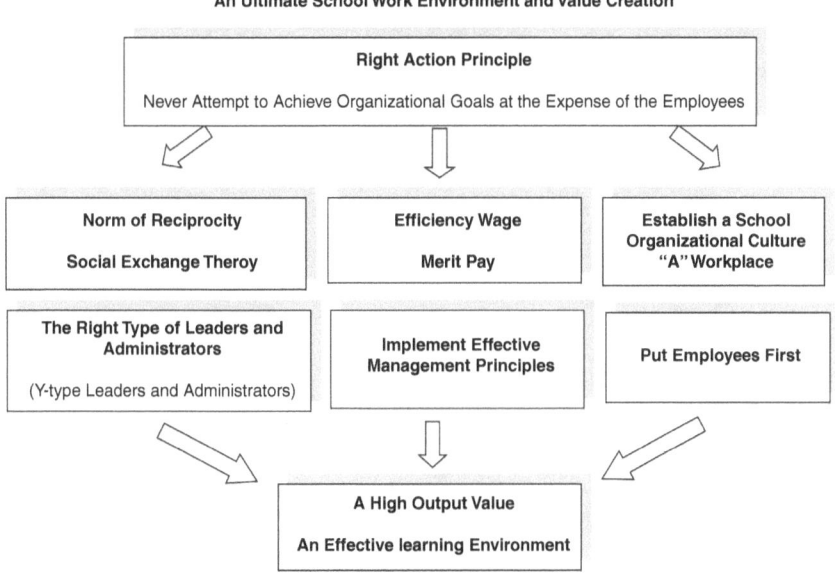

An Ultimate School Work Environment and Value Creation

www.ingramcontent.com/pod-product-compliance
Lightning Source LLC
Chambersburg PA
CBHW021801230426
43669CB00006B/158